Lacrosse Legends of the First Americans

Lacrosse Legends

of the FIRST AMERICANS

Thomas Vennum

The Johns Hopkins University Press
BALTIMORE

© 2007 The Johns Hopkins University Press
All rights reserved. Published 2007
Printed in the United States of America on acid-free paper
9 8 7 6 5 4 3 2 1

The Johns Hopkins University Press
2715 North Charles Street
Baltimore, Maryland 21218-4363
www.press.jhu.edu

Library of Congress Cataloging-in-Publication Data
Vennum, Thomas.
    Lacrosse legends of the first Americans / Thomas Vennum.
        p.   cm.
    Includes bibliographical references and index.
    ISBN-13: 978-0-8018-8628-7 (hardcover : alk. paper)
    ISBN-10: 0-8018-8628-7 (hardcover : alk. paper)
    ISBN-13: 978-0-8018-8629-4 (pbk. : alk. paper)
    ISBN-10: 0-8018-8629-5 (pbk. : alk. paper)
    1. Indians of North America—Folklore. 2. Indians of
North America—Sports. 3. Lacrosse—United States—History.
4. Legends—United States—History and criticism. 5. United
States—History. 6. United States—Folklore. I. Title.
    E98.F6V46 2007
    796.34′708997—dc22
                        2006035479

A catalog record for this book is available from the British Library.

Illustrations on pages 17, 49, 65, 97, and 131 are courtesy of
Tracy Thomas of the Wolf Clan of the Mohawk Nation

To Syracuse coach Roy Simmons Jr.,
friend and legend himself, a constant inspiration and source
of lacrosse knowledge, with a rich supply of his own tales

Contents

Plates follow page 96

Acknowledgments

The following individuals have been helpful at various stages in the preparation of the manuscript: the Al Brown family, Bob Brugger, Josh Christian, Carol Clark, Kip and Matt Dooley, Don Fisher, Tim Galaz, Justin Giles, Sean Hartofilis, Jim Leary, Nancy Lurie, Cesare Marino, Joe Mills, Lewis T. Moran, John Nichols, Glenn Perkins, Anthony Perna, Guha Shankar, Roy Simmons Jr., Lou Stancari, Larry Whalen, and Nat Wheelwright. Particular thanks for their critiques go my sister, Margie Daly, and my former student, Edward Brown. I am especially grateful to the staff of *Inside Lacrosse* magazine for their attention to the Native game and support of my column, "The Indian Pocket."

Lacrosse Legends of the First Americans

INTRODUCTION

What can Indian stories tell us about the game of lacrosse as played by its creators, the first Americans on this continent? The history of this important game has received minimal attention from sports historians, who have instead focused at length on what they perceive as the main "American National Games"—baseball, basketball, football.

The people who invented and first played lacrosse had no written language, so everything about its early history—rules of play, modes of manufacturing game equipment—was transmitted by memory through oral tradition. We probably will never know the origin of lacrosse. The few written accounts from early explorers and missionaries in the so-called New World take us back only a few centuries, although it is probable the game existed in several forms long before "the European invasion" of North America. Some tribes insist they originated lacrosse or were the first to have received it as a gift from the spirit world. A Fox (Meskwakie) legend, for example, tells of a spirit coming to the Indians with a lacrosse stick in one hand, a red, buckskin-covered ball in the other. The spirit is said to have told them the game would belong only to the Fox tribe and that other peoples would have to learn from them.

The American Indian ball game played with a curved, netted stick that we know today as lacrosse in its many variant and descendant versions (box lacrosse, men's and women's field lacrosse, etc.) was widely played throughout the eastern half of North America when Europeans arrived. Consequently, every Indian society in which the game was found had its own name for the sport in the indigenous language. Translated into English, it may have been simply "ball game," "stickball," or "ball-play." (I have used *lacrosse* generically, no matter what the tribe or specific variation in its manner of play.)

In considering the following thirteen stories from oral traditions of five different tribes, the reader should be aware that traditional Native American stories fell into various categories, as they do in any culture. What scholars of the past commonly lumped together as "myths" are now recognized as having important distinctions, even as the word *myth* has generally come to mean something untrue or imagined.

With increased research and linguistic analysis, folklorists have been able to perceive important differences between Indian tales. There are, for instance, what the Ho-Chunk (Winnebago) call *waika* ("what is old"). These are stories belonging to various clans or medicine societies and can only be told in winter. Because they are generally set in primordial times and explain how certain things came to be, they are considered sacred. Their leading figures are supernatural beings—celestial creatures, such as the personified Sun or Moon—or various culture heroes and tricksters, who are recognized as role models and glorified for their deeds. Ho-Chunk "legends," by comparison, are set in a particular time and place and involve specific humans who either encounter or perform something extraordinary. They are "supposed to be true," although some in their native audience may or may not accept them wholesale and might be totally skeptical.

These distinctions are general, and folklorists accept that much depends on the circumstances surrounding the telling, who is the audience, and who is the narrator. Furthermore, a particular story may have characteristics of more than one of the classifications mentioned above. The narratives presented here represent examples of all three categories, although to avoid confusion I have termed them *legends* generically throughout the text.

This rich body of oral literature strongly suggests that lacrosse was played in native North America long before early-seventeenth-century Jesuits in Huronia (present-day southeastern Ontario) gave it the French name we know today. The French word *lacrosse* was unfamiliar to other early travelers

Selected Algonquian Language Words for Lacrosse

As can be seen, all these words are constructed from a basic morpheme meaning "to hit." To simplify comparison for general readers, I have omitted (important) linguistic diacritics that would be meaningful only to linguists.

Language	Tribal location	Word			
Ojibwe	Western Great Lakes	*BA*	*GA'A*	*TO*	*WE*
Pottawatomie	Kansas; Wisconsin	*PE*	*KI'*	*TWE*	*WIN*
Fox (Mesquakie)	Iowa	*PA:*	*KA HA*	*TOWE:*	*WA*
Plains Cree	Manitoba, Canada	*PA*	*KA HA*	*TO*	*WAN*
Nippising	North of Québec	*PA*	*KA*	*TO*	*WIN*
Kaskasia Illinois (ca. 1720)	Mississippi River on the Missouri-Illinois border	*PA*	*KI*	*TA*	

and explorers in the New World, who took the time to record what they saw being played. While native languages were still alive, Indian people used a variety of (mostly) descriptive terms for the sport, which referred to the physical act of playing the game, like the Onondaga *dehuntshegwaes* ("they [men] hit a round object"), or the Ojibwe *bagaa'atowe* ("they hit something") and its variants in other Algonquian languages.

The ancient legends that Native Americans passed down represent an important source of information about all aspects of their cultures, including their games. Handed down over generations, the stories served as the repository of tribal histories; they deserve close examination for clues about lacrosse traditions, many of which have disappeared. A history of the game is virtually impossible to understand without attention to what these legends can offer.

Only recently have sports historians and anthropologists focused on Indian lacrosse. Some of the evidence they have uncovered is meaningful only with recourse to the legends. In these tales the ancestral Native Americans incorporated instructions on "proper" modes of conduct, through examples provided by the behavior of mythical tribal heroes (such as the Iroquois peacemaker Hiawatha). The legends also enabled elders to clarify for the younger generations certain peculiarities in the natural world, such as why the bear's foot is turned in, as explained to children in the legend of "Iena, the Wanderer," where a small boy in a hurry to dress puts his left moccasin on his right foot by mistake.

Large bodies of such legends were the property of the "medicine man," or conjurer—a revered elder responsible for certain traditional lore of a tribe's culture. Among his many duties was maintaining tribal history. The Ojibwe *kanawencikewinini* (literally, "preserve-man") did so with the aid of pictographs (drawings) incised onto birchbark scrolls, and their secret meaning could only be interpreted by him and initiates to the medicine lodge (*mitewiwin*).

The word *medicine* in Indian culture requires explanation, for it has a special meaning beyond pills and soothing liquids. Indian medicine encompasses those physical substances and a wide range of herbal medicines in healing or curing illnesses, but the term has a deeper, more spiritual meaning and was used to describe a wide range of powerful, supernatural means to effect changes—for the better or worse. "He has strong medicine" to any Indian person means that someone has powers, usually hidden. He is able to make things happen beyond the capacity of the average person, things we might assign to the category of magic, such as the power to control weather, causing it to rain or stop raining. In lacrosse, through rituals the medicine man was able to prepare his team to avoid injuries and beat their opponents. Such a person with "medicine power" often was feared because he could bring harm or injury to his intended victim.

Just the phrase "medicine man" conveys a stereotypical image in the white imagination—a spooky, sinister figure, huddled over some sick person on the ground, possibly shaking a rattle while working his incantations, his fingers busily fondling tiny figurine fetishes or maybe even snake vertebrae, or preparing lotions or potions (hence he is sometimes referred to as "conjurer").

The vague notions about Indian medicine men that whites harbor are in fact partly correct. That individual (women could also fill the role) was believed to possess certain supernatural powers; consequently, he played an important, revered, and even feared role in Indian society. His powers were exclusive to him. Among them was voyeurism, the ability to foretell future events and results, for which reason he often accompanied war expeditions. He was capable of seeing at a distance to ascertain the location of lost objects. John Mink, an Ojibwe medicine man on the northern Wisconsin Lac Court Oreilles Reservation in the 1940s, once was able to locate lost car keys for some white tourists who had left them on a tree stump near where they had picnicked on the reservation. Like a doctor in white society, the medicine man also had a vast knowledge of the natural world and could prescribe ingredients to effect cures for a wide range of afflictions.

Because of his powers, the medicine man could work evil as well as good. In this sense he had his counterparts in other traditional cultures, such as in Haitian Vodou. The Haitian equivalent of American Indian medicine man, called *ougan*, was said "to work with both hands" (*travay ak de men*). Because he had such strong powers, he was treated with great respect, and one was often cautioned to "keep your distance." When the great religious practitioner and singer Eniwube (Sits Farther Along) of the Lac du Flambeau Ojibwe in northeastern Wisconsin died sometime after 1911 he was considered to have been so powerful that the women traditionally assigned to clean the body for burial waited three days before daring to enter his house!

Many practices of the former native lacrosse game derived their meaning and intent from the legends retained in the memories of American Indian medicine men. Until recently, for example, in pre-game preparations traditional Cherokee lacrosse players in North Carolina observed a number of restrictions called *gaktunka* (taboos) and followed unusual practices under the guidance of a medicine man ("ole conjure man," he was called) (figure 1). This knowledgeable elder functioned much like a coach and oversaw all aspects of the game, from his selection of players to their training for a game. Because lacrosse has such strong spiritual roots among the Cherokee, the conjurer's instructions were followed rigidly—every much as some practicing Catholics attend Mass and confession, or Orthodox Jews adhere to kosher dietary rules.

Most important, the conjurer knew how to use plants and animals from the natural world in supernatural (magical) ways. Traditionally, the Cherokee believed that certain substances possessed supernatural powers that could help lacrosse players strengthen themselves and avoid game injuries. Only the conjurer knew which ones and how to prepare them (see chapter 4 sidebar). He also could instruct magical means to inflict harm or injuries on members of the opposing team. One of these required preparing a special liquid (made by boiling the left hind leg of a rabbit in water), then finding the path the opposing team would take to the ball field, secretly spilling some of this liquid at various places along the way. Should a barefoot player from the other team unknowingly step on the rabbit-leg potion, when he was about to

FIGURE 1.

An Eastern Cherokee "conjure man" (in background), supervises his players' "going to water" ritual in late 1946 in western North Carolina. In his hands are his divining beads, which he consults to eliminate weak players who might risk being hurt in the game. Players have wild turkey feathers tied into their hair, believed to provide them long-windedness and running capacities. They dip their sticks into the sacred waters of the Oconoluftee River, thought to impart its strength to the sticks.

Photo by Loomis Dean; courtesy of Life *magazine, ©Time Warner, Inc.*

score during the game, his leg would suddenly cramp up and prevent him from succeeding. Many uninformed Euro-Americans still dismiss such practices as examples of "witchcraft" and attribute them to superstitions of Indian people—just another reflection of their "primitive" culture.

The rabbit-leg preparation owes its origin to one of the best-known Indian lacrosse legends—the story about the mythical lacrosse game between the birds and the land animals (chapter 1). In one of several Cherokee versions of the story, the rabbit severely injured his left hind leg while playing for the animals and since then has never been able to use it. Cherokee elders explain to their grandchildren that is why the rabbit leaves only three footprints in his tracks when he runs through the snow. Therefore, the specially prepared liquid transfers the wound from the rabbit leg to an opposing lacrosse player, causing his leg to cramp up at a crucial moment in the game. Without reference to the legend, of course, creating a special "rabbit soup"—an aggressive mechanism to keep opponents from scoring—makes no sense.

Unfortunately, few Indian legends, like the colorful rabbit-leg story, are familiar to nonnative audiences. Sadly, most Americans know relatively little about our native Indian cultures apart from their stereotypical portrayals in television and films. The image presented is difficult to erase. Because its portrayers continue to draw from the same pool of stock attributes, over the years they have created a monotypical, almost "mythical" image of the warrior figure carrying a spear atop a white stallion and inevitably wearing the splayed eagle-feather warbonnet—an icon frequently emblazoned on jerseys of white athletic teams. In truth, this stereotypical image depicts only a tiny percentage of Native Americans in a restricted time-frame (the nineteenth century) and geographical location (the Northern Plains).

By creating the stereotypes, the media have mostly ignored important distinctions between Native Americans of different tribes. Take, for instance, house types. The cone-shaped tepee has come to serve universally as a cultural icon for traditional Indian dwellings, although it hardly represents the many different dwellings evolved by Indians to take advantage of the natural materials available and to deal with the various climates and seasonal changes they lived in. Adopted primarily by tribes living on the Plains, the tepee was the ideal structure for the nomadic existence of peoples who needed to pick up and move at a moment's notice under threat of attack or to pursue buffalo herds.

Because of the tepee stereotype, nonnatives are less familiar with the oblong bark wigwams of Woodlands peoples in the Great Lakes area, or the permanent, rectilinear, multistoried pueblo buildings of adobe and the octagonal *hogans* of the Navajo in the Southwest, the semisubterranean cedar-plank houses of the Hupa in northern California, or the enormous, beehive-shaped grass lodges of the Southern Plains, such as the Wichita constructed.

Pervasive stereotypes tend to portray Indian people as being culturally static, which is far from the case. Like all human societies, the traditional cultures on the North American continent at the time Europeans arrived had been undergoing change for centuries and would continue to do so. Given the natural forces of culture contact, there were constant variations in dress, house styles, customs, and even languages due to intertribal exposure resulting from trade, warfare, and intermarriage. Scholars are constantly challenged to describe such cultural exchanges because of the absence of documentation, which written records, photographs, recordings, or surviving artifacts would provide.

Most newcomers to "the New World" considered the games of lacrosse they encountered to be barbaric and unregulated, thus undeserving of the detailed attention customarily paid the gentlemanly sports of Europe. Following the arrival of Europeans, lacrosse—an Indian invention—was taken over by the white man, along with other Indian inventions such as the snowshoe and toboggan. At the same time, in the two-way street of cultural exchange, several European games were incorporated into daily life of Indian people. American artist Charles Deas painted a game of checkers under way in a Ho-Chunk wigwam in 1842. (For Deas's depiction of an Eastern Sioux lacrosse game, see figure 11.)

Borrowed technology and adaptation is apparent in the construction of lacrosse equipment. When nonnatives adopted the Indian game eventually they abandoned the Indian lacrosse balls traditionally made from rawhide, wood, or baked clay and substituted ones made of hard India rubber. By the early twenty-first century, the curved, webbed racket of wood and rawhide had been replaced with one having a titanium handle and a head with plastic webbing.

Relatively little has survived of traditional Indian sports equipment or athletic apparel to adequately describe the Indian game. Because lacrosse sticks and balls were made from natural materials, very few of them have lasted. Manufactured of hickory or ash wood and strung with rawhide, exposed to the elements they disintegrated over time to become one with the earth. Distinguished players were even buried with their sticks to take with them to "The Hereafter," where, according to Indian beliefs, they could happily continue to play lacrosse forever. (The Abenaki in northeastern Maine point to the flickering Northern Lights as showing the action in a game played by the spirits of their ancestors.) The relatively few old sticks around occasionally turn up in antique shops. (Former Syracuse coach Roy Simmons Jr. has built up his collection of old Iroquois sticks from garage sales!) Conceivably, some sticks in poor shape might even have been burned for kindling in times of stress. Although we can safely assume the game was played for centuries before the arrival of Europeans, the oldest surviving depiction of a lacrosse stick is dated 1790, while the oldest museum examples are from the 1820s.

And what can we really say about the sticks that *have* survived? How can we say for certain that a design element found on one old Indian lacrosse stick speaks for anything more than the individual taste of its particular owner? Like other cultures, Indian people were accustomed to decorate many material objects in everyday life, including their weapons of warfare and their game equipment. In doing so, often they "personalized" such decoration.

Adaptations to the standard Indian lacrosse stick are not restricted to decoration. Of all parts of the stick susceptible to individual "tampering," the head was the obvious candidate. It is well known that white players have forever been adjusting the runners and molding the heads of their sticks using the fist, in an attempt to create a deep and stable pocket. Once plastic heads came on the scene, some players would wrap the mesh tightly around a ball, tie it in that position, and bake the head in an oven to make the deep pocket permanent. Such "tampering" is now illegal and if discovered in unannounced stick-checks by the referees can result in a penalty.

Players seemed less interested in adjustments to the shaft and frame, especially after they began being mass-produced in the 1970s. Whereas the plastic heads—frame, webbing, and throat—could be stamped out as a single unit by machinery, the only "improvement" on the handle or shaft was in strengthening it. Formerly made of hickory and subject to splitting or breaking, these wooden handles were replaced with ones made of metal, at first aluminum and later on titanium.

Given the durability of metal it was perhaps inevitable that this material would eventually be incorporated in lacrosse-stick making, once it was no longer in native hands. Europeans brought with them to North America a

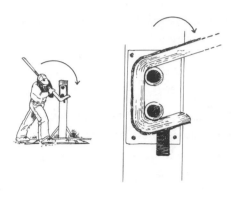

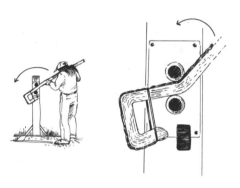

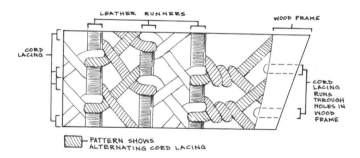

FIGURE 2.
The standard construction of the Iroquoian stick, following the practices of Onondaga traditional craftsman Alfie Jacques, using a specially made steel plate as a fulcrum. Prior to contact with Europeans, Indian stick makers would wrap the steamed, pliable hickory blank around the circumference of a young tree to effect the bend. Inset shows detail of the traditional stringing on the Iroquoian stick.

Drawing by Daphne Shuttleworth

wide array of items made from metal. Indians were quick to perceive the advantages of more durable metal tools and implements than those made of natural materials they had been accustomed to using over the centuries. Indians recognized that the potential life span of a tin pail vastly exceeded that of the traditional Indian bark container; two or three hefty strokes with a hammer on a metal nailhead or a few twists of the wrist with a screwdriver to connect sections of wood were far simpler and the results stronger and longer-lasting than aboriginal techniques of fastening together pieces of wood with wooden pegs.

In 1997, when filming craftsman Earl Nyholm, a master Ojibwe birchbark canoe builder, I made certain to focus on the various implements that Earl snidely referred to as "white man's 'cheater tools,'" while grudgingly acknowledging their effectiveness. The most recently "invented" of these was a small Exacto knife with a retractable blade. He found this tool useful to accomplish a small incision in some difficult-to-reach corner of his work. Whenever I show the film to a white audience, inevitably as Earl reaches into a paper hardware-store bag to retrieve a nail he needs to pound through the gunwales "sandwiching" the birchbark canoe pieces together, someone will blurt out, "He's cheating, he's using nails! That's not Indian!"

Nonnatives need reminding that once Indians were exposed to European craft technologies, they perceived immediately some of their advantages over traditional aboriginal practices. Take the hammer, for instance. Indians had no trouble recognizing that a handle with a solid metal striking surface at its end could focus repeated impacts onto some small surface, such as a nailhead; this had many advantages over clutching a small rock to impart the blows.

Recognizing the longevity of metal, Indians began using this "new" material in fashioning traditional articles—ceremonial rattles, for instance. In the Oklahoma Creek Stomp Dance, a long line of dancers follows a leader who sings brief snippets of a song in a call-and-response manner with the line advancing behind him, "stomping" vigorously. As part of their ceremonial dance attire, participants traditionally wear large tortoise shells strapped to the calf of each leg; the shells are filled with pebbles for their rattling elements. Because almost all American Indian singing is performed to percussion accompaniment, the turtle shells here provide the necessary rhythmic underpinnings to the song. As the destruction of turtle habitat created a shortage of shells, Creek participants began to substitute large, empty condensed-milk

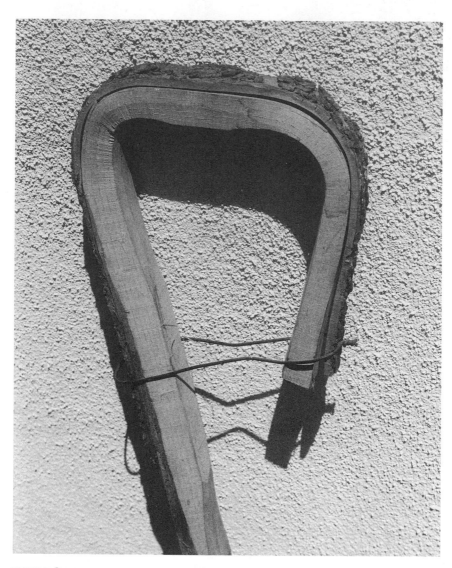

FIGURE 3.
Iroquois hickory lacrosse stick in early stages of construction prior to the removal of the bark. Made by Frank Benedict of the St. Regis Mohawk reservation on the Canada-U.S. border. After steaming to make the wood pliable, the bend is held in position by a loop fashioned from a coat hanger. The stick is allowed to dry for six months, after which the bend will be permanent.

Photo courtesy Timothy Galaz

cans as more durable and available. However, some of the more conservative, traditional Stomp Dance grounds, wishing to adhere to the age-old custom, frown on the practice and post a stern warning on the entrance to the grounds: "no milk cans!" Elsewhere in North America, metal containers were used for rattles. Among Woodlands tribes, leaders of religious ceremonies substituted small condensed-milk cans for aboriginal bark or gourd rattles. The Ho-Chunk neighbors of the Ojibwe in Wisconsin jokingly accused the Ojibwe of using empty beer cans as medicine rattles!

Metal was eventually incorporated into one step of Indian lacrosse-stick making. Craftsmen still making the traditional Iroquois hickory lacrosse stick have created a plate, cut and welded together from pieces of steel, to form a mold and used to bend the hickory shaft at two places, one at the very end which gives the stick its distinctive curved shape at its termination and the other at the neck or throat of the stick (figure 2). After the hickory blank has been steamed to make the wooden fibers pliable, the maker inserts the wood into the mold, then grabbing the free handle for leverage, he can easily force the wood to shape. Once the bends have been created, a metal loop made from a coat hanger is slipped up to hold the two bends in the desired shape, and the stick is put aside to dry for six months, after which the bends will be permanent (figure 3).

The time it takes to construct lacrosse sticks figures in several of the stories here. Those few craftsmen still practicing the craft are greatly admired by their people, for whom the game is still a cornerstone of their culture. The high regard in which Indians held lacrosse is nowhere more evident than in the legends that relate heavenly phenomena to the game: equating a pale moon with a lacrosse ball stuck in the sky because of some contestant's unfair style of playing, or during a thunderstorm interpreting the lightning as the path of the ball as it is passed among the thunderers. Thunder itself is considered to be the sound of the game in the upper world, where spirits play their game in the thunderhead. The Potawatomi of Wisconsin believe that in the Village of the Dead there is no illness or trouble, everyone is happy, and one can play lacrosse forever. Indian people believed the spirits above to be responsible for giving man his lacrosse equipment, leaving behind the first lacrosse ball in a nest high up on a cliff, or causing lightning to strike a tree and make black marks to indicate where one should carve in making the lacrosse stick.

Even in legends where lacrosse is not the principal focus, the ball-play is

The map shows the locations of lacrosse legends presented here approximately at the time they were told to (or translated for) the collectors. Tribal locations on the map reflect federally enforced Indian relocations onto reservations, often far away from original homelands, which may have been where the tales originated.

(1) The Great Game in Which the Birds Defeat the Quadrupeds (Eastern Cherokee)
(2) A Dog's Power Beats the Old Chief (Seneca)
(3) The Pale Moon (Eastern Cherokee)
(4) Playing with an Evil Head (Seneca)
(5) The First Lacrosse Ball (Menominee)
(6) Playing for Heads (Seneca)
(7) Wakyabide Is Killed Playing Lacrosse, Later Takes Revenge (Ojibwe)
(8) The Warriors of the Ho-Chunk Nation Struggle on Home Turf (Ho-Chunk)
(9) He Who Wears Human Heads as Earrings Defeats the Giants (Ho-Chunk)
(10) Manabus Is Dogged by Waves (Menominee)
(11) Why the Turkey Buzzard Has a Red Scabby Neck (Ojibwe)
(12) Snakes around the Neck (Oklahoma Cherokee)
(13) An Unusual Penalty Box (Seneca)

Map by Bill Nelson, after a map drafted by Lewis T. Moran

always portrayed as part of the typical Indian landscape. In the following passage from the Ottawa legend of O-na-wat-a-qut-o (He That Catches the Clouds), the hero gazes through a hole in the clouds looking down onto earth: "He saw below the Great Lakes and the villages of the Indians. In one place he saw a war party stealing on the camp of their enemies. In another he saw feasting and dancing. On a green plain *young men were engaged at ball.* Along a stream women were engaged in gathering the *a-puk-wa* [reeds] for mats" (emphasis added). In the Ojibwe legend of "Kwasind, or the Fearfully Strong Man," the action takes place in *bawitig* (present-day Sault Ste. Marie) at the east end of Lake Superior. The tale describes it as a village "where the young men amused themselves very much in ancient times in sports and ball-playing."

We owe much to scholars in the field who took the trouble to write down these legends as dictated by traditional storytellers. Folklorists, anthropologists, and linguists collected them at a time when Indian traditions were changing rapidly, becoming absorbed into American culture. By the end of the nineteenth century, many native languages and practices were rapidly disappearing, following efforts to absorb "the vanishing American" into mainstream society. We can assume that the legends had their origins in the precontact period, when Indian societies were relatively intact, that is, as yet "uncontaminated" by Euro-American influences. However, by the time the stories were collected in the late-nineteenth and early-twentieth centuries, traditional Indian culture was in shatters. Indians had been devastated by European diseases (especially smallpox), been defeated militarily, and had their lands taken from them. Forced to live on small reservations and deprived of former pursuits such as hunting buffalo or gathering wild rice, they found themselves competing in a market economy.

Although the basic plots of the legends may be aboriginal, the stories were flexible enough to incorporate certain factors contemporaneous with the time of their telling. Details in the action of some stories give clear evidence that they were collected after contact with Euro-American culture. For example, the goals of the lacrosse game described in "Manabus Is Dogged by Waves" (chapter 4) are located at Chicago and Detroit, cities only settled after the westward expansion of Europeans. The appearance of the term "inning" in one legend could only have occurred after Indians had been exposed to American sports. Indeed, Indians themselves were quick to take up baseball and form teams. The influence of white religion is also apparent in the use of such words as "Creator," although Indians themselves had equivalents of this figure, frequently "the Great Spirit."

Some of these legends were published in collections along with other stories from the same tribe; others were left as field notes in anthropological archives. In some legends, lacrosse is the main focus; in others, the sport is played as a fragmentary episode in the course of a much longer string of some hero's adventures.

How accurately were these texts recorded? Before tape recorders were available, Indian legends were dictated to the collector in the field, and most stories went through a third party—the interpreter translating them from the native language. When the collector published them, he sometimes omitted what he considered repetitious or unimportant passages. He also may have shortened or "cleaned up" passages he judged offensive to his audience. Some collectors even combined several versions of the same story to provide "the full tale." (In a few places in this collection I have judiciously edited wording to bring it up to date, for example changing "he bethought himself of" to "he remembered.")

With these cautions in mind, lacrosse enthusiasts can enjoy these traditional tales, gaining insight into the spiritual world of Indian peoples. They can picture the stage setting, which the inventors of the sport designed for their lacrosse heroes—animal as well as human—to compete in the often violent contests of the distant past. Today's players can appreciate how lacrosse became the vehicle by which Indians captured an important British fort in the mid-eighteenth century; they will also come to recognize that in these "great games" the stakes were enormously high, and that defeated teams could often quite literally "lose their heads."

1

ANIMALS AS STAR PLAYERS

Indians believed that in mythical times animals and humans freely inter-
mixed, including playing games together. Consequently, in legends people
and animals often take each other's roles: creatures talk and behave like
human beings, and humans occasionally possess animal attributes, like the
ability to fly.

These old beliefs are slow to die. Traditional Ojibwe still believe that bears
are the closest animals to humans and can understand their language. (They
point to the piteous humanlike cries of bears when caught in a trap and their
clever capacities to elude hunters by jumping from tree stumps to avoid leaving a trail.) These beliefs explain the existence of stories where animals play
lacrosse just like humans. Possibly the oldest legend in the present collection
is the "Great Game" between the birds and land animals. The story is widely
known, having crossed linguistic and cultural boundaries between Indian
peoples whose traditional homelands are widely dispersed in North America.* Elements of the story also appear in Indian legends which focus on other
aspects of lacrosse.

---

*See, for example, the Mohawk version of "The Great Game" in *tewaarathon (Lacrosse): Akwe-
sasne's Story of Our National Game* (North American Indian Traveling College, 1978), 8.

By relating the game as taking place in the mythical past, one can easily imagine the narrator beginning the story by saying, "Once upon a time . . . " or something similar. Having the game played only by the creatures of the wild in effect suggests the very antiquity of lacrosse in the Indian mind— a sport possibly even existing before man had appeared on Mother Earth. Indian people in North America have never been as obsessed as Euro-Americans are for having "all the facts" about how things began and developed, so the origins of the game are left happily vague and obscure. It is enough that younger Indian generations know that in the distant past lacrosse was played by the ancestors of all the animals they were familiar with. It may be implicit that at some point the creatures taught the Indians how to play, but that would be another story.

The Great Game in Which the Birds Defeat the Quadrupeds (Eastern Cherokee)

Leaving the question of "origins" unresolved, there are many examples of how the game was initially played by animals and birds. The version of the legend below was collected by the researcher James Mooney from Eastern Cherokee in western North Carolina and published in the *American Anthropologist* in 1890 as part of his larger study, "The Cherokee Ball Play."

The Eastern Cherokee are that branch of the tribe living in western North Carolina. With more than 300,000 today identifying themselves as Cherokee, they form the largest federally recognized tribe in the United States. At the time of contact with Europeans, the Cherokee were scattered over approximately 40,000 square miles in eight present-day states of the Southeast. In the Treaty of New Echota (1838), a reservation was created for them in Indian Territory (Oklahoma), where they currently occupy fourteen counties in the northeastern part of the state. Eventually 7,000 federal troops were sent to enforce Cherokee removal. To avoid moving, some Cherokee claimed North Carolina citizenship or hid out in the Great Smoky Mountains. The descendants of those who remained in North Carolina make up the Eastern Cherokee. To maintain cultural and linguistic ties with those who moved west, they have, since 1984, met in joint sessions with the Oklahoma Cherokee.

The Cherokee are unique in having had their own writing system. It was developed by Sequoyah, who was the first in history to delineate a written language without being literate in at least one language. Using eighty-five symbols to represent vowel/consonant combinations, the writing system was immediately put to use printing hymnals and religious tracts as well as newspapers.

The collector of this legend, James Mooney (1861–1921), is unquestionably the foremost of the many scholars whose research contributed to the present book. Mooney's Irish heritage made him particularly sympathetic to the plight of Native Americans. His interest in the Eastern Cherokee was initiated by meeting their "chief," N. J. Smith, at the Bureau of American Ethnology, where Mooney worked. He had been allowed to "sit in on" interviews with Smith and take notes on Cherokee vocabulary and grammar. When he began fieldwork in western North Carolina, Mooney gained the confidence of his informants by immersing himself totally in their culture. On his first research trip to the Eastern Cherokee in the summer of 1886, he began collecting plants used by medicine men and learning their specific applications. He developed a close working relationship with the medicine man, Swimmer, who was probably the informant who assisted Mooney in his investigation of the traditional ball game and who may have told him the legend of the great game between birds and animals.

On his second field trip he took a camera and became the first in 1888 to take lacrosse photographs. Complaining that Henry Schoolcraft's six huge volumes on the American Indian (1851–57) contained less than two pages on Indian ball games, Mooney wrote in great detail about the sport. He was struck by the fact that it was unimportant who won or lost but that the centrality of lacrosse to Cherokee culture was reflected in the mythology and the ceremonialism surrounding the game. In 1890, the same year his lacrosse study was published in the *American Anthropologist,* because of the threat of further Sioux uprisings following the Wounded Knee massacre, Mooney was en route to research the Ghost Dance religion at Pine Ridge Agency in present-day South Dakota.

According to a Cherokee myth, the animals once challenged the birds to a great ball play. The wager was accepted, the preliminaries were arranged, and at last the contestants assembled at the appointed spot— the animals on the ground, while the birds took position in the tree-tops to await the throwing up of the ball. On the side of the animals were the bear, whose ponderous weight bore down all opposition; the deer, who excelled all others in running; and the terrapin, who was invulnerable to the stoutest blows. On the side of the birds were the eagle, the hawk, and the great *Tlaniwa*—all noted for their swiftness and power of flight. While the [birds] were pruning their feathers and watching every motion of their adversaries below, they noticed two small creatures, hardly larger than mice, climbing up the tree on which was perched the leader of the birds. Finally they reached the top and humbly asked the captain to be allowed to join in the game. The captain looked at them a moment and, seeing that they were four-footed, asked them why they did not go to the animals where they properly belonged. The little things explained that they had done so, but had been laughed at and rejected on account of their diminutive size. On hearing their story the bird captain was disposed to take pity on them, but there was one serious difficulty in the way—how could they join the birds when they had no wings? The eagle, the hawk, and the rest now crowded around, and after some discussion, it was decided to try and make wings for the little fellows. But how to do it! All at once, by a happy inspiration, one remembered the drum which was to be used in the [ball-game] dance. The head was made of ground-hog leather, and perhaps a corner could be cut off and utilized for wings. No sooner suggested than done. Two pieces of leather taken from the drum-head were cut into shape and attached to the legs of one of the small animals, and thus originated *Tlameha*, the bat. The ball was now tossed up, and the bat was told to catch it, and his expertness in dodging and circling about, keeping the ball constantly in motion and never allowing it to fall to the ground, soon convinced the birds that they had gained a most valuable ally.

They next turned their attention to the other little creature; and now behold a worse difficulty! All their leather had been used in making wings for the bat, and there was no time to send for more. In this dilemma it was suggested that perhaps wings might be made by stretching out the skin of the animal itself. So two large birds seized him from opposite sides with their strong bills, and by tugging and pulling at his fur for several minutes succeeded in stretching the skin between the fore and hind feet until at last the thing was done and there was *Tewa*, the flying squirrel. Then the bird captain, to try him, threw up the ball, when the flying squirrel, with a graceful bound, sprang off the limb and, catching it in his teeth, carried it through the air to another tree-top 100 feet away.

When all was ready the game began, but at the very outset the flying squirrel caught the ball and carried it up a tree, then threw it to the birds, who kept it in the air for some time, when it dropped; but just before it reached the ground the bat seized it, and by his dodging and doubling kept it out of the way of even the swiftest of the animals until he finally threw it in at the goal, and thus won the victory for the birds. Because of their assistance on this occasion, the ball player invokes the aid of the bat and the flying squirrel and ties a small piece of the bat's wing to his ball stick or fastens it to the frame on which the sticks are hung during the dance.

Source: *"The Cherokee Ball Play,"* American Anthropologist *3 (1890): 105–32. Another version of the legend is James Mooney, "Myths of the Cherokee,"* 19th Annual Report of the Bureau of American Ethnology, *part 1 (Washington, DC: Government Printing Office, 1900), 286.*

The story emphasizes playing skills and physical characteristics crucial to winning lacrosse games. On the animal side, the deer is useful because of its great speed as a runner. The terrapin is a valuable teammate because his thick shell makes him immune to the many blows from opponents' sticks, and the bear, given his "ponderous weight," is equipped to barge his way through a line of defenders. These skills are matched by the birds' principal advantage, their "swift flight" and maneuverability, talents that allow them to elude quadrupeds pursuing them and move quickly to other parts of the field out of danger. But, as the story makes clear, it is principally the addition of two new players to the birds' team—the flying squirrel and the bat—that gives them the victory. The birds enable the squirrel to be airborne by stretching the skin between his forelegs and hind legs, and they change a mouse into a bat by providing a pair of wings. With their valuable new allies, the birds' side wins. The bat turns out to be an essential player through his ability to keep the ball aloft at all times, never letting it fall to the ground where the animals might retrieve it and score.

There is considerable irony in this legend, which is told by many southeastern tribes including the North Carolina Cherokee. If keeping the ball airborne is seen as a valuable skill, it would suggest that the style of lacrosse playing depended on accurate passing. However, the southeastern game uses two sticks, so the passing abilities so crucial to today's field game are almost nonexistent. In fact, the ball is on the ground a considerable amount of time when southeastern tribes play.

STYLE OF PLAY

Unquestionably the most difficult aspect of traditional Indian lacrosse to describe with any certainty is the technique of play. There are few published reports or manuscripts that provide detailed assessment of stick handling or ball control in historical American Indian lacrosse. Most of what we know comes from historical photographs, published and manuscript descriptions, and judicious guesswork based on the examination of old sticks in museum collections and personal family archives.

A few old action photographs are of some, but not much, help. Certain written accounts are useful, such as George Beers, who formulated the rules of lacrosse in 1869. He contrasted Indian and Canadian techniques of play, but even some of Beers's descriptions are sketchy. For instance, what does Beers mean by the term "frisking," apparently a common Mohawk technique in mid-nineteenth-century Canada? The most that can be gleaned from his description is some sort of maneuver by a player to retrieve a ground ball with the feet (hands, of course, were disallowed). Apparently, "to frisk," the player uses his heels to capture the ball, then jumps up with the ball held between his feet. While still airborne, it seems, he kicks the ball up behind him, simultaneously twirling around to catch it with his stick in mid-air. Beers does not indicate when or why a player would "frisk" the ball, except to surprise opponents, and the practice seems to have been abandoned long ago. (Interestingly, a similar trick is still common among today's soccer players, who also are not allowed to use their hands.)

It is difficult to perceive changes in Indian playing techniques over time. The Great Lakes version of lacrosse virtually died out by about 1950, while the Iroquoian game, the progenitor of today's field lacrosse, seems to have kept pace with modifications of "the white man's" game. It was certainly affected by rule changes outlined in regulation manuals beginning in the nineteenth century, when Indian teams regularly began to compete with their Canadian counterparts. Perhaps only in the southeastern two-stick version of the game does there seem to be any sort of unbroken tradition, especially among tribes transplanted to Indian Territory in the 1830s and playing today in Oklahoma. This seems true also for descendants of those who stayed behind in their traditional homelands and have perpetuated or revived the traditional form of the game. North Carolina Cherokee and Mississippi Choctaw are two examples.

The earliest sources on lacrosse, the Jesuits in Huronia in the 1630s, tell us nothing about the sticks or how they were used. The natural tendency for newcomers to North America in describing lacrosse to their European audiences back home was to compare it to European games they were familiar with. This is of little help to us today; in fact, their reports although old, are often misleading. For instance, one analogy was to the game of tennis. The tennis comparisons led some sports historians to add something about lacrosse to tennis histories, like William H. Maddren's five-page "history" of lacrosse, appended to J. Parmly Parets's *Lawn Tennis: Its Past, Present, and Future* (1904). Apparently these writers accepted unchallenged as sources of information the observations of early explorers in the New World, such as Peter Martyr in his *De Orbe Novo* (1511–30), where he stated that "Indians love games, especially tennis," a comparison later repeated by Jonathan Carver (1710–80), explorer in the Great Lakes, and Jean-Bernard Bossu (1720–92) among the Choctaw. The tennis comparison suggests that what they saw might have been Indians using their sticks to bat a ball. But comparing lacrosse to tennis, a game invented by French clergy and nobility in the thirteenth century, is inaccurate (although in 1992 Seneca Indian player Linley Logan recalled practicing as a youth, using tennis rackets when lacrosse sticks were unavailable). In order to actually bat a ball, a player's webbing would have had to been much more taut than the open network found on the typical northeastern stick—although some sticks are more tightly woven than others, such as those of the Passamaquoddy (see figure 4). And as early lacrosse sticks lacked any guard-strings, running with the ball must have been a balancing act.

Both sports use a racket with webbing and a small ball, but why Europeans would see Indian lacrosse as anything like tennis is puzzling. A one-on-one game, usually confined to a small court, tennis most often involves only two players batting a ball over a net. By contrast, Europeans observed hundreds of Indians roaming on a large playing area, probably carrying or at least throwing a ball toward goals placed on either end of the field. Europeans also compared what they saw to a variety of other familiar games, many of them forms of stickball: bandy (field hockey), shinny, or, as Englishman John Law-

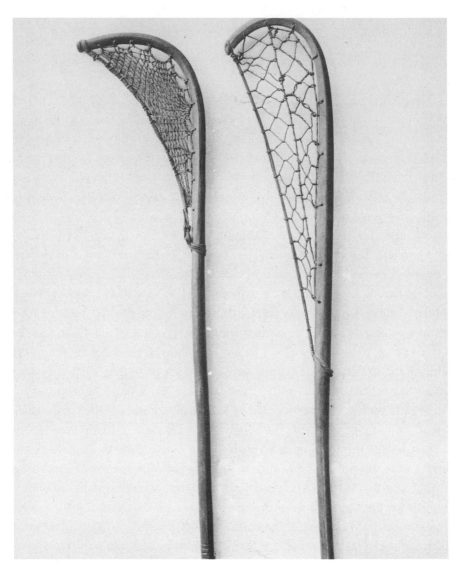

FIGURE 4.

Two contemporaneous northeastern sticks. Pre-1872 Passamaquoddy stick from Pleasant Point, Maine (*left*), next to a pre-1875 Mohawk stick from the St. Regis (Akwesasne) Reservation (*right*). Note the unusually dense webbing of the Passamaquoddy stick.

Photo courtesy of the National Museum of Natural History, Smithsonian Institution son wrote in his *History of North Carolina,* a game "managed with a Batoon and a Ball, [which] resembles our Trap-ball."* Another writer compared lacrosse to "battledore and shuttlecock," an early form of badminton.

Based mostly on the sticks and balls, we can distinguish three quite different versions of Indian lacrosse (northeastern, Great Lakes, and southeastern). The southeastern game by far has been the best documented for the longest period of time and appears to have changed little for nearly 300 years. Between the detailed paintings of noted ethnoartist George Catlin (1796–1872) from the 1830s, the photographs and published works of James Mooney (ca. 1890) and the thorough analysis of the Cherokee game by anthropologist Raymond Fogelson in 1962, we have a reasonably clear picture of the style to describe in general terms its techniques of play, at least for the nineteenth and twentieth centuries.

THE SOUTHEASTERN STICK

The greatest difference of the southeastern playing style is the use of two sticks, one held in each hand, functioning like extensions of the player's arms. In the Great Lakes or Northeast, by contrast, the player used both hands on the stick's handle. Southeastern sticks are considerably lighter in weight and their frames more fragile than those of the sturdy northeastern or Great Lakes sticks. They are constructed from hickory blanks in pairs two- to two-and-a-half-feet long, with the cup on the end of one stick made slightly smaller than the other to fit inside it and secure the ball (figure 5). (These oblong, tear-shaped cups to many early writers suggested ladles; see plate 6.) During play the southeastern player holds the sticks close to his body to keep the ball between the sticks (figure 6).

Historically, many Indian players made their own sticks. Length depended on the man's taste or what position he played. Like many material items in traditional Indian culture, the maker used parts of his body for measurement, so there is little uniformity from stick to stick. Just as a Great Lakes canoe-builder spaced his boats' ribs on the span between his thumb and forefinger or drilled holes on the cedar flute, locating them where the player's fingers naturally fell, a Cherokee Indian explained that the ideal length of the

---

*John Lawson, *History of North Carolina* (1714; 3rd ed., reprint, Richmond: Garrett and Massey, 1937), 186.

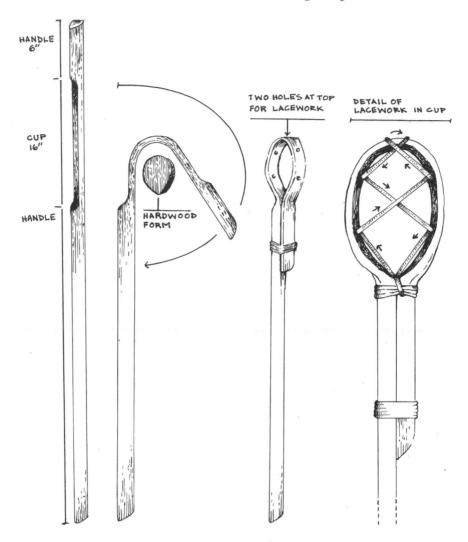

FIGURE 5.

The standard construction of one of a pair of southeastern sticks.

Drawing by Daphne Shuttleworth

southeastern stick was the distance from the player's fingertips to the ground, when his arms were relaxed by his side (see plate 5).

The lacing on the cup was minimal, because of the small size and light weight of the ball. Only two strands of lacing were used for a pocket—formerly animal skin or twisted bark, today made of commercial leather. This rather

feeble network frequently broke during a game, so there were always replace-
ment strings on the sidelines. That such a stick could be easily crafted on short
notice is suggested by an anecdote in the historical lore of lacrosse. During
the Civil War, in 1863 a group of Cherokee Confederate volunteers are said to
have been bored with their assignment guarding a bridge in Tennessee. They
decided to play lacrosse. Lacking sticks, they made them on the spot, using
bark for their lacing.

How does the southeastern player handle his sticks? To recover a ground
ball, he uses a sort of pincer maneuver to capture the ball between the ends
of the two cups. Given the stick's construction, the thin end of the cup and the

FIGURE 6.
A young Choctaw player from Philadelphia, Mississippi, shows how a pair of southeastern
sticks are used. The ball-carrier runs with wrists crossed to secure the ball between the
tear-shaped cups of his sticks. Players in bare feet wear cut-off jeans for a game on their
high school football field.

Photo courtesy Kendall Blanchard

way it is laced, there is no way to "shovel" the ball, as with the northeastern stick, or to scoop it, as with the Great Lakes stick. Once the ball is contained within the two cups, to run or pass with it the player uses the sticks as arm extensions. In running, he crosses his wrists in a kind of clamp to keep the ball firmly captured between the void and webbing of the two cups.

Actual passing is virtually nonexistent in the southeastern game. Usually a player simply throws the ball downfield in the general direction of the goal in hopes that a teammate can recover the ball from the ground. What may look like a passing attempt is usually just a maneuver to get rid of the ball quickly when one is heavily defended. A player being dogged will bring the two sticks up over his shoulder, perhaps take a few preliminary steps in the direction of the goal, then usually leading with his foot he turns sideways with his full torso and throws the ball over and out, simply by unclamping his sticks to release the ball. He then follows through with the right leg. Because accuracy is rarely achieved in this manner, calling this "passing" would be a misnomer. If a ball carrier finds himself hemmed in by opponents he might rid himself of the ball by resorting to this overhead throw, in which case he turns outward from the circle of opponents while simultaneously leaping up to release the ball over their heads. Of course, in doing so he runs the risk of having an opposing player grab him from behind with an arm (not an infraction in the southeastern game), and pull him over, in which case he might try to fire off a shot while still upright, or even from a kneeling position.

Anyone familiar with field lacrosse is immediately struck by the apparent lack of teamwork or strategy evident in the southeastern game. The ball, which is on the ground most of the time, makes very slow progress. Scarcely larger than a golf ball and covered with some natural animal skin in a color close to that of the grass (which on the field is rarely cut), the ball is difficult to spot on the ground. This has given rise to one strategy—deception in ball-handling. Because most on the field, including referees, have likely lost track of where the ball really is, a player can easily fake possession by running with his cups clamped together and acting as a decoy to relieve pressure from the teammate who actually has the ball.

FIELD ACTION

On a typical southeastern field, six to eight players might have formed a tight circle somewhere near where they think the ball may have landed, crowding together with yelling, jostling, flailing and banging of sticks in an attempt to come up with it. American traveler and landscape painter Charles Lanman in 1848 described the typical Cherokee pile-up as "a dozen gladiators, striving to overcome a monstrous serpent." If one has successfully retrieved a ground ball, he attempts to break open from what looks more like a rugby scrum than a team effort. Captain Basil Hall, a British naval officer and traveler, watching a Creek game in 1828 gave this report of the gauntlet awaiting the player who breaks away: "At length, an Indian more expert than the others, continued to nip the ball between the ends of his two sticks, and, having managed to fork it out, ran off with it like a deer, with his arms raised over his head, pursued by the whole party engaged in the first struggle. The unfortunate youth was, of course, intercepted in his progress twenty different times by his antagonists, who shot like hawks across his flight from all parts of the field, to knock the prize out of his grasp, or to trip him up—in short, by any means to prevent his throwing it through [the goal]."*

In the southeastern game, those used to today's regulation field lacrosse are struck immediately by its "no-holds-barred" nature. Any sort of physical action required to stop an opponent's progress and dislodge the ball from his possession seems to have been tolerated in the southeastern game: there were no rules against tripping, ramming, wrestling, choking, holding, or slashing (see plate 4). In his research on Eastern Cherokee lacrosse, anthropologist Raymond Fogelson once took part in one of the practice sessions. He found the exercise utterly exhausting due to the energies expended in holding his opponent or freeing himself from the opponent's clutches—interspersed with the periodic sprinting required in scoring.

"BOSS" ANIMALS

The story of the great game among animals is unique among lacrosse legends presented here in that no humans take part. For story purposes, each animal—Hawk, Terrapin, Eagle—should be taken to represent an entire species. Indians believed that every creature on earth was merely a representative of the "king," or spiritual head of the species. This "boss" of the species had put his representatives here on earth to help man: their meat provided him with

*Basil Hall, *Travels in North America in the Years 1827 and 1828* (Edinburgh: Cadell, 1829), 3:302.

food to appease his hunger; their fur gave him warm clothing and bedding; their feathers and tails he could use as body decorations.

Traditionally, when an Indian needs any of these creatures, it is customary for him to petition the boss spirit of the animal, give prayers, and usually offer tobacco in gratitude. The practice of tobacco offering also extends to plants: whenever a canoe-builder strips bark from a birch tree to make a canoe, he deposits a small token tobacco offering at the foot of the tree before departing. When one goes to hunt deer he must first petition the head spirit of that species, Deer, who like all spirits resides in the heavens; afterward, in his feast with the animal's flesh, he gives thanks to Deer with his tobacco offerings.

Beyond this Cherokee tale, animals continue to play major roles in lacrosse legends, but typically interacting with humans. In mythical time, it was believed, humans and animals communicated with each other, thus they engaged in sports together. The southeastern story of the great game between the birds and the land animals is one of the few legends to omit any human involvement in the game—the bat and flying squirrel are the real stars of the action.

A Dog's Power Beats the Old Chief (Seneca)

A legend collected by Jeremiah Curtin and J. N. B. Hewitt from the Seneca in present-day upstate New York assigns the role of star to another creature—a dog, who is interceding on behalf of humans. Where the game in the Cherokee legend was initiated with a challenge from the birds, in the following story the game is proposed by an evil chief (a human) in a string of challenges attempting to take the life of a young man. Having lost to him at foot-racing, the chief next proposes they compete in lacrosse. The dog, disguised as the young man's brother, takes his place in the game and wins. That particular creature, as we shall see from this tale, has a very special place in Indian beliefs and practices.

The Seneca are one of the six nations forming the League of the Iroquois. The territories of the nations making up the Confederacy are conceived of as forming a geographical longhouse (the traditional bark wigwam-like structure used for religious ceremonies) across present-day northern New York State. The Seneca are considered to form the "western door" of the longhouse, just as the Mohawk represent its "eastern door." At the time of contact with Europeans, the Seneca practiced agriculture supplemented with hunting and fishing. They successfully resisted French efforts to gain their territories in the seventeenth century and later joined the British against the United States. In retaliation, U.S. general John Sullivan and his troops burned their crops and villages as they moved across upper New York State. Through a series of treaties the Seneca gave up their former territories and moved onto three reservations created for them near Buffalo while some settled with other Iroquois on the Six Nations Reserve in southeastern Ontario. They practice the longhouse religion based on the visions of Handsome Lake, himself a Seneca.

John Napoleon Brinton Hewitt (1850–1937), the son of a Scottish father and Tuscarora Indian mother, worked as photographer and linguist for the Department of Indian Affairs. He was fluent in three Iroquoian languages (Tuscarora, Mohawk, and Onondaga) and published extensively. Hewitt was particularly noted for helping establish a relationship between the Cherokee and Iroquoian languages. A tireless researcher, at his death he left behind 12,000 pages of an unpublished manuscript.

Born in Wisconsin around 1835, Jeremiah Curtin was a folktale collector and linguist. As a Harvard undergraduate, he studied languages outside the curriculum, including Hebrew and Gaelic. Having mastered Russian, Curtin in 1864 was appointed by President Lincoln as secretary of the American legation to Russia and traveled extensively in Eastern Europe, Asia, and Ireland. Working as an ethnologist in the Bureau of American Ethnology from 1883 to 1891, he published twelve volumes of oral traditions and legends. Curtin specialized in Seneca culture and legends of the Creek and Wintu Indians, among others.

When the old man came home he said to his son, "I thank you for outrunning your enemy, the Chief; there has never been anyone who could outrun him; all have been beaten. Since the wager was your heads, you can take his life whenever you wish." The old man then asked his son whether he had done his best.

"No," said he, "I only used about half my strength."

"Very well," said the old man, "the Chief has another game to propose. He will never stop proposing trials of strength, skill, or speed until he has taken your life. To have been beaten by you in running this time makes him very angry, so in two days he will challenge you to play lacrosse against him."

"All right," replied the son, "I am ready to meet him."

In two days they saw the Chief coming. As he entered the lodge, he said: "I am dying for a lacrosse game, and I challenge you to play a game against me; you won in the running game, now try another. I will wager all I have, and if you win, you will be chief in my place."

The son replied, "I, too, am bored from lack of amusement, so I accept your challenge. I have never met the man who could beat me in a lacrosse game. But you must give me time. You have come unexpectedly, and I must make a ball club [lacrosse stick]."

"Very well," said the Chief, going away.

The bent wooden ball club frame the hunter hung up to season, while the old man cut strings from rawhide; the next day they netted the club. They were ready just in time to go to the lacrosse field. The time appointed for the game was at midday, and the old man and woman said, "We shall start now."

"Very well, I shall come soon," said their son.

Then the little dog said, "Why don't we have our eldest brother take part in this game instead?" So the son removed his garments, and the dog put them on; there he stood, looking just like the son, as though he were his older brother.

"Now," said the little dog, "we shall surely win the game."

The hunter and the other dogs went to the woods to hunt, while the dog-man went to the ball ground. The Chief was already there, watching impatiently for his opponent, when at last he saw him coming. With his long hair tied back, he carried his club well and looked splendid. The old man, believing that it was his son, said, "Now you must use all your strength and must not be beaten." The dog-man saw that his antagonist was walking around in the crowd, with a very proud and haughty manner. By comparison, the dog-man seemed to the people very mild and without strength enough for the game.

Seeing that it was time to begin, the people moved back to give room to the players. When the word was given, the players came forward, and the Chief said: "I will take my place on this side." "No, you shall not," said his opponent. "You gave the challenge, so I will choose my place." The Chief had to yield, the dog-man choosing the side the Chief had wanted. Then they began to play.

"Now," said the little dog to the hunter in the woods, "our brother has begun the game, which will be a very close contest." Soon he reported, "The Chief's ball has missed the goal; they play well; our brother has caught and sent the ball back. Oh! Now he has won an inning. They will play one more inning." All at once he called out: "They have begun again. It is a very close game, our brother is having all he can do. We may be beaten, however." Then he called out, *"Owe! Owe!* our brother has won the game." He turned to the old man's son saying, "You are now chief, and all the old Chief has belongs to us."

The dog-man had won two straight games, so he caught the Chief by the hair and cut his head off. Many of the people thanked him. They said that the old Chief had never spared them; that whenever he had been the loser, he had always given the people up to slaughter and saved his own life. The winner seemed to have won many friends among those who witnessed the game. The little dog said: "Now we shall go home." They had been there but a short time when the winning ball-player came in; giving back the son's garments, he immediately became a dog again.

When the old people came into the lodge, they thanked their son, saying, "You have done more than anyone else was ever able to do before. You are the Chief now." Even while they praised their son, they did not know that it was a dog that had done the work.

The next morning the little dog said, "Let us go to live in the Chief's lodge." So the hunter, with the old man and his family, moved into the new lodge. All the old Chief's things had been left in their places, as they were part of the wager. Now, because the dogs were so full of *orenda* [power], the son became a great chief and had much power and influence among the people.

Source: *J. Curtin and J. N. P. Hewitt, "Seneca Fiction, Legends, and Myths," in the* Twenty-eighth Annual Report of the Bureau of America Ethnology *(Washington, DC: Government Printing Office, 1911), 234–36.*

This legend of the Seneca of upstate New York demonstrates Iroquoian beliefs about the supernatural powers (*orenda*) of dogs. The main character in the story is a dog who takes the form of a human to play lacrosse against an evil chief. He is able to defeat him, thereby allowing a new chief to take his place, moving into the old chief's house and gaining all his possessions. The story also makes clear that a lacrosse game provided an important gambling outlet for American Indians.

Legends in many world cultures describe such demonstrations of athletic skill in challenges back and forth between the central characters. In a Ho-Chunk (Winnebago) legend the hero, Red Horn, and his companions enter into a series of contests against the giants, beginning with a lacrosse game in which the giants are defeated (see chapter 4). Then they challenge each other to see who can shoot the farthest, stay underwater the longest, then win in a dice game. Red Horn and his companions are finally defeated in wrestling and are killed. The final prize, or wager, in these contests is usually something very important—in the evil chief story the winner can take the loser's life by cutting off his head.

Footraces between the major characters are common in many Indian legends. A story of the Assiniboine in Manitoba tells how Fox, pretending to be lame, is challenged to a race by Inktumni, their trickster-hero. To make the race fair, Inktumni ties a stone to his foot. Of course, Fox outruns Inktumni and eats all his food. The contests also involve a certain amount of back-and-forth boasting, just as there was between the Ho-Chunk Manegi (*manegi her-era,* Those Who Live on Earth) and Wangeregi (*wangeregi herera,* Those Who Are Above) teams.

Like many stories, this Seneca legend has a happy ending. The old people think it was their son playing, so they congratulate him on becoming the new Chief. The little dog reminds them they can now go to live in the old Chief's lodge and take over all his possessions "left in their places" as part of the reward for winning. Because the dogs were rooting for his side all along, through their power the new Chief becomes "great" and rules his people, having enormous influence on them.

THE DOG IN INDIAN BELIEFS

Indian legends take place in mythical time, so the dog, although disguised, is able to take the role of a human lacrosse player. Being a particularly potent creature, he is of course able to defeat the Chief, who thinks all along he is playing against the old man's son.

If the Chief had known he was actually to compete with a dog, it is doubtful he would have agreed to the game. In American Indian beliefs generally, and Iroquoian beliefs especially, dogs are seen as having special powers. Anthropologists tell us that dogs in American Indian cultures fall into a "liminal" category, that is, they exist in a borderline area between common, everyday life and the sacred, religious, or spiritual realm.

On the one hand, Indian dogs lived a miserable existence. Anyone who has spent time on an Indian reservation has experienced how dogs, unless they are cared for as pets, are considered dirty, unwelcome nuisances to be kept out of doors. Subject to kicks, blows from sticks, and other physical abuse, mixed-breed curs must survive off whatever scraps of food they can scavenge. Traditionally, Indian peoples considered dogs such dirty and lowly creatures that their presence at some religious function was thought to have a contaminating effect. Formerly, dogs of the Ojibwe that wandered into and interrupted a medicine dance would be taken out and strangled on the spot!

On the other hand, some Indians considered dogs to be potentially powerful creatures that deserved special treatment. As the Seneca narrator of this legend told anthropologists Curtin and Hewitt, "Dogs still know all we say, only they are not at liberty to speak." He also stressed their potential danger if treated badly: "If you do not love a dog, he has power to injure you by his *orenda*."*

Not only were dogs significant actors in tribal stories like the Seneca legend, as spiritual creatures they also had certain rituals based on their actions and ceremonies in which they played a central role. For instance, the now-extinct Begging Dance, practiced by both the Sioux and Ojibwe as a form of "trick-or-treat," was designed to force stingy members of the tribe to bring out food. Participants in the Begging Dance party were said to represent a band of dogs going from lodge to lodge. Their performance was seen as a reenactment of the story in which a boy who had been left as a newborn outside among the dogs leads them from camp to camp soliciting food in return for singing. One singer, Eniwube, from the Lac du Flambeau Ojibwe Reservation in northeastern Wisconsin, preceded the melody of one song by actually barking like a dog in his performance of special begging dance songs recorded onto wax cylinders in 1911.

The belief systems of Iroquoian tribes, including the Seneca, recognized the liminal place of a dog. For the New Year's or Midwinter ceremony, two completely white dogs were selected to serve as sacrificial messengers to the Great Spirit. Being white, they were considered to be proper creatures to be used as sacrifice—that is, they were "pure" and without blemishes. The two dogs were carefully strangled to avoid breaking any of their bones, then they were hung at the top of a pole for a time before being brought down and

---

*J. Curtin and J. N. B. Hewitt, "Seneca Fiction, Legends, and Myths," in the *Twenty-eighth Annual Report of the Bureau of American Ethnology* (Washington, DC: Government Printing Office, 1911), 236.

burned. In the Ottawa legend of "Onaizo, the Sky-Walker," a white dog is killed and roasted as a sacrifice to save the life of a child, whose parents requested the feast.

An ornamental carving on the tip of one Iroquoian lacrosse stick made sometime before 1845 demonstrates the association of dogs with lacrosse (see figure 9). Currently in the anthropology collections of the University of Pennsylvania Museum in Philadelphia, the stick was made by the grandfather of Alexander T. General, a Cayuga Indian living on the Six Nation Reserve in Ontario, across Lake Erie from Buffalo, New York. The elaborately carved stick probably was never played with but was simply handed down as an heirloom in the General family. There are no scratches or nicks on the hickory shaft that would indicate it had seen action, nor is there the usual dark patina that one finds on handles of old sticks, where the player's dirty, sweaty hands had grasped it during games. Also, a few animal hairs are still attached to some of the rawhide webbing. Normally, if the stick had been used in games these hairs would have rubbed off. It was probably too important an icon to be subjected to the roughness of a lacrosse game.

GAMBLING AND LACROSSE

The central concern of the Seneca players is whether the Chief will be killed and his opponent, the son, will take his place. Not surprisingly, this extreme form of wager—having one's head cut off resulting from a lacrosse loss—has never been reported in the human world. However, other enormously high stakes, including betting one's wife and children on a game, were at one time acceptable practice.

The rapid spread of casinos on reservations since the late twentieth century reflects how various forms of gambling have been common in American Indian cultures for centuries. Lacrosse matches were no exception. Even the earliest reports from Europeans in the New World confirm that Native Americans bet on lacrosse games. Jesuits among the Huron Indians in the 1630s noted rematches being planned to recoup betting losses from earlier lacrosse games. They reported that the wagering would become desperate, as the amount of the bets became increasingly higher.

Indian lacrosse games involving betting have become part of the lore of the sport. Vital to American history was the game played in 1763 at Fort Michilimackinac, where Lower Michigan today joins the Upper Peninsula by bridge.

The game was a crucial event in the so-called Pontiac Wars and led to the Indians' occupation of the fort. During the Pontiac Wars, the Indians and their French allies defeated the British in a string of takeovers of fur-trading posts and forts, including Detroit.

On June 4, 1763, the Fox (Mesquakie) played the Ojibwe in an exhibition game staged outside the fort's gates to celebrate the English king's birthday. Secretly, the Indians had planned the takeover of the fort by luring soldiers outside to watch the game. British noncommissioned officers familiar with the violence in English football would have been especially anxious to see the game. The plan was to keep them distracted, so they would not notice what the Indian women were doing. Pretending to be innocent spectators, the women had weapons concealed under their blankets and shawls. As they gradually gathered at the fort's entrance, they were ready to hand knives and hatchets to the players as they raced into the fort in pursuit of a ball deliberately tossed through the open land-gate.

One means of keeping the soldiers focused on the game was to encourage them to join in the wagering on the contest, just as they saw all the Indian spectators doing. Although it is not recorded historically, it is plausible some of the bets were between British soldiers and native spectators. With a personal stake in the game's outcome, a soldier would have noticed nothing unusual about the quiet movement of Indian women wrapped in blankets, inching back into the fort with their hidden weapons. His eyes would have been glued to the violent action of this unusual New World sport—perhaps his first chance to see it up close.

Missionaries opposed gambling of any sort, and they were particularly upset by the wagering on lacrosse games and couldn't understand why Indian religious leaders accepted the practice. Not only was the betting "sinful," driving Indians further into poverty, games usually interfered with Indian attendance at church services. Missionaries frequently joined forces with government officials to bring an end to Indian gaming. Such official opposition happened on the Nett Lake Reservation in northern Minnesota in 1920, when a prohibition against the Ojibwe moccasin game was enacted. Before then, small groups of Indian men in their leisure hours would bet on a team's success in discovering under which of four moccasins the opponents had hidden a marked bullet. The stakes wagered on the game were often high.

Community lacrosse games were always major Indian social events; well planned and advertised in advance, they would draw large crowds, especially when one nation played another. A reported 10,000 attended a game where the Creek played against the Choctaw to settle a boundary dispute. Like summer powwows today in Indian country, these lacrosse games turned into large social events, bringing together relatives from distant communities as well as urban Indians returning to their home reservations. As these friends gathered, it was natural for some to begin betting on the game's outcome.

How much was wagered on an Indian lacrosse game? A Jesuit report of 1639 claims that a Huron betting on a game might lose in goods or money as much as 200–300 *écus,* apparently a large sum. A century later the practice continued. French explorer Pierre de Charlevoix (1682–1761) related how the Huron would keep raising the stakes "till they have stript themselves stark naked and lost all their moveables [furniture] in their cabbins; some have even been known to stake their liberty for a certain time."*

As extreme as it may sound today, Indians—especially owners of slaves or white captives—considered humans as potential objects to be wagered on a lacrosse game. Leech Lake (Minnesota) Ojibwe Dan White reminisced in 1970 about his reservation's formerly strong lacrosse tradition. The game was so central to everyday life that one of their communities was called "Ball Club [lacrosse stick]." The town, today the site of reservation summer powwows, is adjacent to the shores of Ball Club Lake, where once the Ojibwe played whenever the water receded enough to provide a field. Discussing the gambling that went on, White speculated about wagering humans, "When these people played those games, well, they lost everything they had, even their wives and some of their children at times. I don't know why they put in their wives as betting there, whether they loved the game that much, but I suppose that after the person started losing, why, he tries to see if the luck would change." As expected, the higher the stakes in an Indian lacrosse game, the harder the contest would be played. A former Choctaw player echoed Dan White's feelings: "I think I would have tried harder if someone was betting that much money on me . . . If I had my wife and kids standing out there as my stakes, I would have played like hell."†

*Pierre de Charlevoix, *Journal of a Voyage to North America* (London: R. & J. Dodsley, 1761), 3:12.
†Transcript of interview, Dan White, Leech Lake Minnesota Ojibwe, South Dakota American Indian Oral History Project, University of South Dakota, Vermilion, Tape 279a, pp. 2, 4; Kendall Blanchard, *The Mississippi Choctaw at Play: The Serious Side of Leisure* (Urbana: University of Illinois Press, 1981), 39.

Lacrosse players themselves were deeply involved in the wagering. Among the Eastern Cherokee a player would bet with the opponent assigned to him from the other team, matching the value of some item. One might put up a blanket, expecting his opponent to do the same. Then the two items would be tied together and put alongside other players' bets to await the game's outcome. Because the combined value of all the wagers was considerable, they required securing for the duration of the game; customarily, elders of the tribe were assigned this job. Whenever Ojibwe played each other, the captain of each team would appoint a stakeholder to guard the items bet. To keep track of the wagers, Eastern Cherokee stakeholders had sharpened sticks they inserted in the ground as a means of "registering the bets," which were assembled in a large pile off to one side of the field.

Some communities put up small tents to cover the wagers or, like the Choctaw, placed them on a scaffold opposite the center of the field. Before a Choctaw game, a man on horseback would ride through the crowd collecting items such as handkerchiefs tied together, or securing cash bets in his wallet. The stakeholders were always trusted to remember the amounts of the bets and to distribute the winnings fairly following the game. Other communities had the wagers draped over or tied to a special long "betting pole," or frame. George Catlin painted the action in a Dakota women's game; prominent in the background is a typical wager pole, the length of it filled with brightly colored articles of clothing. A similar pole on the east side of the field was also used to display prizes in the Menominee game sponsored by a dream obligation. The game sponsor awarded goods or prizes periodically during the game. During a break after each goal was scored, the sponsor would take items from the pole to award as prizes for the winners of that period of play. If the game had been sponsored or dictated by the thunderers in the dream, bachelors receiving prizes could donate them to female relatives.

Eastern Cherokee lacrosse preparations were so elaborate that placing bets was made into a small ritual. Each team would line up at its goal with fans behind them; then, carrying the items to be wagered in their hands, they would march as a group to meet the opposite side at midfield, where the actual betting then took place (see plate 2).

Rarely were there disagreements over the bets at a game's conclusion— principally because losers could make up their losses in a rematch invariably scheduled for just that purpose. Rematches were so common that a community hardly ever faced sustained economic loss from lacrosse games. Their players were able to recover what they had lost previously and possibly even increase their winnings. Over time, most losses were balanced out with winnings. Usually losses over lacrosse games took place in a friendly atmosphere. Europeans were always surprised at the stoicism displayed by those who lost. One described a man after the game, having lost all his clothes, leaving for home singing!

Not every game ended peacefully, however, and there are reports of ill feelings getting out of hand. (Oklahoma Cherokee spectators purposely left their guns at home.) After-game incidents of violence have been recorded, particularly when a losing team suspected that their opponents' medicine man might have used magic charms to prevent them from scoring. Bringing in the supernatural to assist in winning was customary with the Cherokee. The ball team conjurer had magic formulas he recited to ensure that the bettors on the other team would lose.

Such beliefs lasted well into the twentieth century. Franklin Basina, a Red Cliff (Wisconsin) Ojibwe, remembered a 1950 game he played in where two old women from the other community were keeping his team from scoring by standing on either side of the goal tossing *jiibik* (magic) balls in the air. A former Mississippi Choctaw player recalled a late-nineteenth-century game where, just as when one side was about to win, a medicine man of the opposing team caused it to rain violently, canceling the game. This provoked a huge fight, with everyone racing to the scaffold to collect the bets wagered, trying to save what he thought belonged to him. In a Dominion Day 1874 game, the Brampton Excelsiors, a British Columbia team, won over the native Six Nations team; a newspaper account describes the game as characterized by much betting and fighting.

Annuity payment times, when the government was required to pay Indians the yearly money owed them from treaty agreements, turned into large social gatherings, celebrated in dances and games. At the 1855 payments at La Pointe, Wisconsin, authorities canceled a planned lacrosse game because so much cash was suddenly in Indian hands. They feared that it would lead to Indians gambling away their money before traders had a chance to collect the debts owed them which had been run up on credit in the winter months.

Eventually unscrupulous whites got involved in managing the operations of lacrosse betting. In some places, they combined their control over the gambling with liquor sales, which often sparked fighting. Inevitably, government authorities got involved. In 1898, for instance, the State of Mississippi outlawed duels, cock-fights, and gambling on Indian lacrosse games. Because the money involved was considerable, it also led to bribing dishonest players to "throw the game."

Gambling, combined with increasing Indian poverty and the opposition of church and government, had a negative impact on Indian lacrosse, leading to a noticeable decline in the native game in some areas beginning about 1900. The funds formerly wagered on Indian lacrosse were forced to find more legal and socially approved outlets than gambling. In some communities like Cherokee, North Carolina, traditional games continued to be staged, often as tourist entertainment. The sponsoring committees in such a case might reward players with prize money.

IROQUOIAN STICKS

In the story we learned that "the bent ball club [was] hung up to dry." Even if we did not know that this legend came from the Seneca, the "bent" stick is a clear cue that its people lived somewhere in the St. Lawrence River Valley, and there was also a good chance the legend originated with one of the six nations of the Iroquois Confederacy. Actually, all traditional wooden American Indian sticks required some bending in their manufacture, but the Iroquois stick above all was characterized by having the upper third of the hickory shaft bent over in a sort of crook. This was accomplished by steam-heating the portion of the stick, which required bending to loosen the wood's fibers (see figure 2), making them sufficiently pliable to take stress without cracking or breaking the shaft. Once the desired bend was accomplished, that part of the stick would be fixed in the bent position and allowed to dry, after which the bend would be permanent. Iroquois stick makers today make a kind of elongated loop from a metal coat-hanger and slip it up the stick to hold the bend in the desired shape, so the stick maker can release the tension used in bending it (see figure 3).

The next step in the construction occurs when it is "hung up to season." It takes about six months for an average hickory stick to dry, at which time it can be released from whatever form or wire loop has fixed the bend in position. (Because the story takes place in legendary time, what would normally take half a year is compressed into two days.) The stick is now ready to have the thick hickory bark removed from the outside of the rectangular, nearly square shaft. After that, with a spoke-shave, plane, or knife, the maker whit-

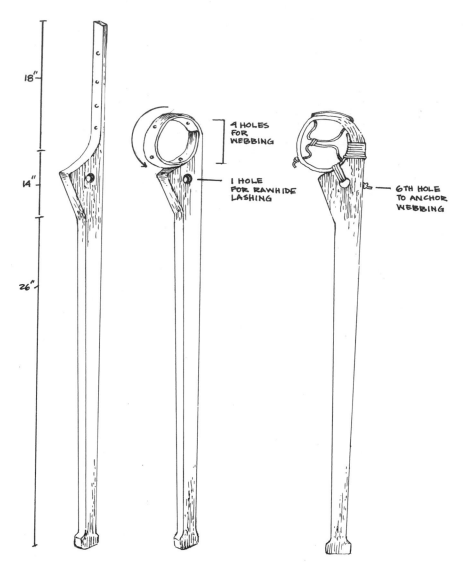

18"

14"

26"

4 HOLES
FOR
WEBBING

1 HOLE
FOR RAWHIDE
LASHING

6TH HOLE
TO ANCHOR
WEBBING

FIGURE 7.
The standard construction of the Great Lakes stick.

Drawing by Daphne Shuttleworth

tles the shaft down to the desired roundness on the handle where a player will hold the stick. The bent portion is thinned out into a somewhat flatter surface where the holes will be drilled at the top of the stick to anchor the top of the webbing, or stringing. Finally, before being strung, the frame is sanded and then lacquered.

"The next day they netted the club." Before the arrival of sticks made from synthetic materials around 1970, rawhide or catgut was sliced into thin strings or strips woven to form a netted surface attached to the frame. Stick making among the Iroquois was a sort of cottage industry, occupying an entire family year-round. In winter, while the women at home usually were doing the stringing, their men would likely be in the woods, selecting more hickory trees to be felled, brought back home, cut into the desired lengths, then split into the right width for the blanks. This was accomplished in winter, when the frozen wood could be split easily.

The open curve, or "crook," in the Iroquois stick's frame is its distinguishing hallmark (see figure 4), and this bent stick is the ancestor of all sticks used in today's field games. The crook in the stick leaves roughly an open V-shape area for the net, which controls the ball, itself considerably smaller than the area of the netting. This contrasts with the stick used west of the Iroquois in the Great Lakes region by Algonquian and Siouan speakers (Menominee, Potawatomi, Ho-Chunk, Santee). Their sticks also required steaming and bending, but the main difference is that the bent portion of the Great Lakes stick is brought completely around and abuts itself, forming an enclosed circle scarcely larger than the ball. Once the circle was created, it was lashed in place with rawhide and allowed to dry in that position (figure 7).

On Great Lakes and southeastern sticks, the cup controlling the ball is completely enclosed by the wooden frame, unlike the Iroquois stick, which, minus its webbing, is open. Whereas the Great Lakes stick features a completely round enclosure, the southeastern stick is more elongated into a tear shape, like an almond. Both the Great Lakes and southeastern sticks had very minimal webbing—usually only a few thongs intertwined and perhaps tied together where they met roughly at midpoint in the cup to form a pocket. By contrast, the Iroquoian and other northeastern sticks were more densely woven—like a spider web or a hairnet.

The "crook" shape of the Iroquois stick is responsible for one nonnative myth that continues to be repeated without substantiation—even recently by such reputable news sources as *Sports Illustrated* and the *New York Times*.

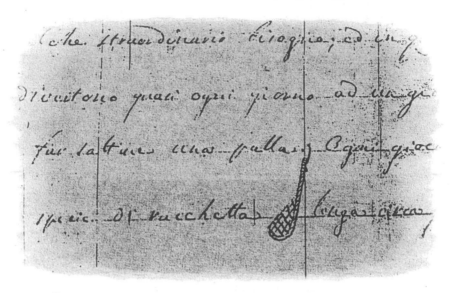

FIGURE 8.

Sketch of an Oneida lacrosse stick in a 1790 diary entry the Italian explorer Count Paolo Andreani, made while traveling in present-day upstate New York. This is the oldest known illustration of a lacrosse stick. The accompanying description reads: "During the months of the harvest this [Oneida] nation does not go out [to hunt], except in the case of some extraordinary need; and during this time the men amuse themselves almost every day at a game which consists of making a ball jump. Every player is equipped with a kind of racket, about 4 feet, 6 inches long, which in the lower end curves considerably; thus resembling the string of a bow, it serves to throw the ball. One who gets to catch it with this instrument and, making it jump in this manner, prevents others from touching it until he can make a determinate number of rounds of a large field, he is the winner. This game requires agility at running and dexterity; and we attended one such game that lasted 2½ hours, during which a great sum of money was bet by both sides. The other amusements consist of running—at times on foot to a certain goal, at times on horseback."

Translation courtesy Cesare Marino; photo by Franco Zaina, courtesy of Laboratorio di Ricerca e di Documentazione Antropologica, Bergamo, Italy; reproduced with kind permission of Countess Luisa Sormani, Milan, Italy

The story is that the French Jesuits among the Huron Indians in the 1630s called the game lacrosse after the bishops crosse, or crozier. Supposedly they saw the resemblance between the Indian stick and the Catholic bishop's tall staff that looks like a shepherd's crook; he carried the staff in processions as his ecclesiastical badge, identifying him as the "shepherd of his flock."

That the "crooked" shape of the traditional Iroquois stick has not changed in more than 200 years is shown by a recently discovered drawing of a late-eighteenth-century Oneida stick. (The Oneida, like the Seneca, are part of the Iroquois Confederacy.) The small sketch was made by Count Paolo Andreani (1763–1823), an Italian explorer in what is central upstate New York today. He made the sketch in his diary in 1790 together with a brief description of an Oneida lacrosse game he witnessed (figure 8). It shows the two principal characteristic features of the Iroquois stick: the bent shaft and dense webbing. It is not known what the spiral wrapping on the shaft is meant to represent.

THE EVOLUTION OF TODAY'S LACROSSE STICK

The stick traditionally used in the northeastern sector of North America and especially among Iroquoian tribes on either side of the St. Lawrence River Valley is the progenitor of all sticks used today in both women's and men's lacrosse, box as well as field. Unlike the Great Lakes or southeastern versions, in its original form which we can now date back at least to the late eighteenth century, the northeastern stick was unenclosed.

Because the end of the crook was left free, the playing surface of the stick was created by running a string from an incision near the end of the crook, about a half inch from its tip, to be anchored in a groove somewhere along the handle, like stringing a bow, but high enough to give the player room to keep both hands on the shaft. This formed a triangle of sorts between the string, the crook, and part of the handle. The triangular area was then filled in (strung) with rawhide webbing to provide the playing surface needed to control the ball.

The design underwent significant changes during the nineteenth century. To discern these, we are fortunate that anthropologist Frank Speck acquired three sticks of the Cayuga Indians, whose manufacture covered three generations of the Alexander T. General [Deskaheh] family; the sticks, as previously mentioned, are currently at the University of Pennsylvania Museum (figure 9). The Cayuga are one of the tribes that make up the Iroquois Confederacy, and the General family lived on the Six Nations Reserve near Brantford in southeastern Ontario. The sticks document the changes in the Iroquoian stick for the period roughly 1840–90. Very likely, there were similar changes in the sticks used by other Iroquoian-speakers, as they surely would have been playing in games with the Cayuga.

In addition to his very own stick, General provided ones his grandfather and father made and played with. Whereas the overall form of the Cayuga stick remained the same over the three generations, there is an evident change in the webbing—a key factor in ball-handling. On the grandfather's

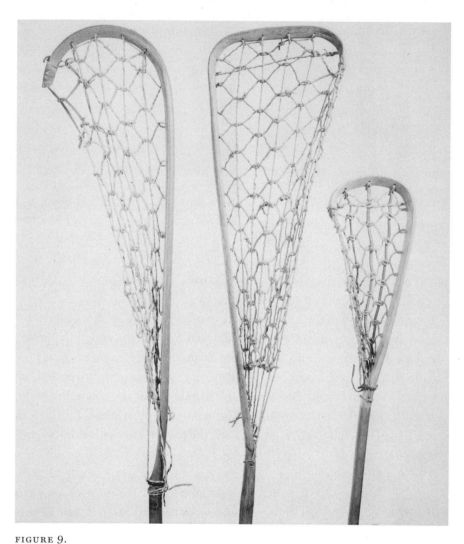

FIGURE 9.

Cayuga sticks made by three generations of the Alexander T. General family on the Six Nations Reserve near Brantford, Ontario. Their manufacture spans nearly a century and documents important changes in Iroquois stick construction, leading to the addition of guard strings and the development of a pocket, reflecting increased participation of whites in lacrosse and their competition with Indians. The sticks date to before 1845 (*left*), before 1910 (*middle*), and 1932 (*right*). The ca. 1910 stick is left-handed.

University of Pennsylvania Museum, Philadelphia; photo courtesy Trustees of the University of Pennsylvania stick, the webbing is woven into a flat surface, with the outermost string on the same plane as the other strings. This raises the question of stick control, for there is virtually no wall to contain the ball, to function as does the pocket on later sticks. In fact, the only wall, if it can even be considered as such, is along the crooked portion of the shaft, which rises a bit above the plane of the webbing and nearly perpendicular to it, but scarcely enough to help keep the ball on the stick. The player using such a stick must have needed considerable balancing skills to maintain control of the ball, particularly in running with it. We should also remember that the balls from that period were unlike today's smooth, round, hard-rubber ball, but more a lightweight deerskin covering stuffed with animal hair, moss, or grass. (Sticks earlier than grand-father General's had more loosely woven webbing, which conceivably made balancing the ball easier.)

The left-hand stick made by Isaac General (Alexander's father) we can take to represent a transitional period—one the Cayuga called "the middle game"—roughly 1860–90. It is a large stick, 4 feet 10 inches in length, meeting the standards for sticks given in the *Official Handbook* (1888). Whites had begun to adopt lacrosse about 1850, when Montrealers "civilized" the Mohawk game they had watched on the nearby reserves. Sticks such as Isaac's were being manufactured for use in regulation play of whites—a commercial market had emerged for the Indian product. (All hickory wooden sticks were manufac-tured exclusively by Indians well into the twentieth century.)

The most significant change the stick shows, however, is its webbing. It lies on a flat plane like the earlier sticks, but provides the first evidence of guard-strings running from the tip of the crook to the handle. (Young players today are puzzled that any lacrosse sticks ever lacked guard strings or gutwalls.) This shows the move toward an actual pocket. The stick has three guard strings at the outermost edge of the webbing, forming at least a sort of pocket, although there is still no "sag" of the webbing near the throat of the webbed surface. Also, the stick is nowhere nearly as "dished" as the modern stick, but it nevertheless appears capable of scooping a ground ball.

Deskaheh's own stick, as collected in 1932, represents another stage in the evolution of the modern stick. Anthropologist Speck was told it represented the "modern" type of Cayuga stick. Also meeting *Handbook* regulations, it is considerably smaller (3 feet 5 inches) than his father's, and the 6 1/2-inch crook is proportionately shorter. The webbing meets the shaft 25 inches from its butt end, providing 10 inches more handle to grip than on his father's stick. The newest feature on the stick, however, is an actual pocket. It retains the three guard-strings and sloped wall of the transitional Cayuga stick, because the guard-strings, formerly left loose, are now woven into the edge of the webbing, providing good sides to the pocket. The webbing also incorporates lengthwise runners made of commercial oil-tanned leather, which are interwoven with the rawhide webbing strings. The pocket on Alexander's stick appears pressed and molded (just as today), probably by the owner's fist. A good picture of sticks from this period (and even earlier) can be seen in a photograph of Onondaga players about 1910—a man (probably Howard Hill) with a left-handed version and John Isaacs with a right-handed stick. The modern features evident on the sticks are the gutwall, shorter handles, and both triangular and rounded crooks, flattened to increase the stick's scooping ability.

The addition of guard-strings, later replaced by a gutwall, went a long way toward achieving a functional pocket. The official handbook required guard-strings as early as 1880. They covered the very tip of the crook, whereas Iroquoian sticks formerly had a slight protrusion beyond the groove anchoring the outermost string of the webbing. This protrusion was useful to hook the webbing of an opponent's stick and jerk it from his hands.

The addition of guard-strings and development of a pocket show the northeastern stick by the 1930s to be approaching its final form, which essentially lasted until the 1970s. That period saw the non-Indian commercially manufactured sticks made of synthetic materials replace the old, wooden Indian crosse, too heavy and difficult to match with a backup stick. The Euro-American designers eliminated the most distinctive feature of the old crosse—its crook—by extending the outer wall of the head completely around, forming a continuous frame to encompass the webbing. The new plastic molded head had evolved into an enclosed frame, just as one found on the Great Lakes and southeastern sticks.

The manufacture of the handsome, traditional Iroquoian stick is now carried on by only a few dedicated craftsmen. Because the traditional stick took a year to make and hickory wood was growing ever scarcer, there was no way the native craftsmen could keep up with the demand for lacrosse sticks, particularly given the explosion in lacrosse popularity in the last quarter of the twentieth century. That period saw the proliferation of stick-manufacturing companies using synthetic materials.

2

GAME EQUIPMENT FROM THE UPPER WORLD

In the beliefs of most tribes playing lacrosse, the game here on earth is the same as played by the spirits who dwell in the heavens. There is a deeply spiritual association of lacrosse with the benevolent deities ruling the universe. This is evident in the Iroquoian belief that, in holding a lacrosse game, the men are "playing for the Creator," and that whoever wins or loses or how many are on a side is immaterial to him. That they are playing is pleasing enough to him.

Indian legends are filled with references to the essential game equipment, whether here on earth or in the heavens. It is in the sky that Northern Lights represent the lacrosse sticks moving in the ancestral Abenakis' games in the heavens, and it is from above the Indians received the equipment they play with in the game. In one story, black marks on the tree struck by lightning guide the maker to show where to cut the wood in crafting the lacrosse stick. If men don't play properly, there are consequences.

The Pale Moon (Eastern Cherokee)

Like the story of the great game between the birds and quadrupeds, this legend (published by jurist and historian John Haywood in the 1820s) also comes from the Cherokee of the southeastern Appalachians, although this tale has a moral lesson. Its very brevity suggests it may represent a condensation of some longer legend.

A self-taught lawyer, John Haywood was appointed to the North Carolina Supreme Court in 1794. He is best known for his histories of Tennessee in which he tried to prove that the tribes of the state derived from the ancient Hebrews. He made important compilations of the state statutes, and his writings laid the groundwork for the state's first historical society, the Tennessee Antiquarian Society (1820).

> In the time of Te-shy-Natchee, two chiefs made a ball-play, at which all the red people attended, men, women, and children. The contest between the parties was very severe for a long time, when one of them got the advantage by the superior skill of a young man. His adversary on the other side, seeing no chance of success in fair play, attempted to cheat, when in throwing the ball, it stuck in the sky and turned into the appearance which the moon hath, to remind the Indians that cheating and dishonesty are crimes. When the moon becomes small and pale, it is because the ball has been handled by unfair play.

> Source: *John Haywood,* The Natural and Aboriginal History of Tennessee *(Nashville: George Wilson, 1823), 267.*

In Indian beliefs, the sky is the realm of the supernaturals, and many things visible in the heavens, such as various star formations, are explained as reflecting the behavior of the gods. For instance, some tribes interpret lightning as the motion of the ball in the game the supernaturals are playing in the thunderhead.

Given the sacred nature of the game to Indians, it is not surprising to find a legendary association of the lacrosse ball with a heavenly body—the moon, in this case. In the same work, Haywood wrote that the Cherokee at one time believed that the moon presided over the lacrosse game as its tutelary spirit and protective guardian; for this reason, in ancient times the Cherokee only played games during a full moon. Such beliefs suggest the very antiquity of lacrosse.

This pale moon legend explains the origins of the moon and its phases from a moral point of view. The change in the moon's appearance is meant to remind humans that cheating in a lacrosse game is wrong. "Unfair play" is displeasing to the sky spirits, and they let humans know this by transforming a celestial object in a way that is apparent to all who view it.

THE INDIAN LACROSSE BALL

Indian lacrosse balls were more than simple spheres thrown from sticks to score goals. The great attention to their manufacture and special uses show balls to be just as important as sticks in the ancient inventory of lacrosse equipment.

All known traditional Indian balls were of one of two types: the first was a solid, round, hard sphere carved from wood or formed from clay and baked hard, then perhaps covered in skin. This type of ball, now extinct, was mostly used in the Great Lakes area, where the round pocket on the sticks was only slightly larger than the ball. Just as the sticks of the Southeast had only enough webbing to prevent the ball falling through the tear-shaped pocket, the minimal rawhide thong webbing across the Great Lakes pocket was merely sufficient to keep the ball from slipping through the cup. The second type of ball, still being manufactured, is a lightweight, roundish bag of some sort, made entirely of strips of animal hide or skin exteriors with some soft material packed inside (moss, grass, animal hair). The covering would be sewn shut after being stuffed, or, in the case of the bag, closed with a drawstring. Some balls were made entirely of skin strips. William L. Stone in his classic *Life of Joseph Bryant* (1838) describes the Iroquoian ball as formed of a network of woven thongs of untanned deerskin, "strained to the tension of tight elasticity." Similarly, the exterior of the Choctaw ball was woven of latticework buckskin strips and stuffed tightly with punk, moss, or deer hair. As the latticework cover dried, it compressed the interior material and became very hard.

Lacrosse balls were decorated in many ways. The Great Lakes ball might be painted in two halves—one red, the other blue, the choice of colors corresponding to the color scheme found on the drumhead of the ceremonial "Big Drum" of Algonquian speakers (Ojibwe, Menominee, Fox, Potawatomi). The colors had ritual associations: red represented warmth, life, the spring season, and the direction south; blue symbolized cold, death, winter, and north. In ceremonies the drums were ritually prescribed to face these two cardinal directions, with a thin yellow stripe across the diameter running east and west separating the red and blue fields and symbolizing "the path of the sun."

Accordingly, in the Big Drum ceremony, the drum was to be raised on its legs at sunrise and taken down at sunset.

Wooden balls were usually carved from pine knots. The English-Ojibwe dictionary published by Bishop Frederic Baraga (first edition, 1853; new edition, 1878–80) gives *pikwâkwad* as the word for lacrosse ball, synonymous with "knob on a tree." The word is also incorporated into the name of a weapon, *pikwâkwado-pagamâgan*, "war-club with a big knob on the end." These balls were very dense and heavy, the wood selected from knots of the tree where the sap was compacted. Some have holes perforated through them causing them to produce a noise as they traveled through the air—the "whistling ball" of the Great Lakes.

When made of a softer wood such as white willow, the ball might have designs carved into it. The German cartographer Johann Kohl, visiting Lake Superior's Madeline Island in 1855 during government disbursement of the treaty money owed the Indians, hoped in vain to see a local Ojibwe game; unfortunately, the authorities prohibited the Indians from playing, but Kohl was at least able to watch ball makers at work carving stars and crosses into the wood. The meanings of some designs were kept secret, such as those on a ball in a Menominee war bundle belonging to David Amab's grandfather. The ball was painted red and blue, but Amab didn't know, or at least was unwilling to explain to ethnomusicologist Frances Densmore, the meaning of a small black cross on one side of the ball, a white cross on the other.

The manufacture of lacrosse balls was usually entrusted to specialists—most often medicine men or conjurers; among the Mexican Kickapoo, he had to be a member of the eagle clan. The ball was considered capable of supernatural performance, particularly if it had been "doctored" by a medicine man. These practitioners were known to hide things inside the ball at the time it was being made—an inchworm, for example. Supposedly invisible to birds, the hidden inchworm was believed to make it hard for opponents on the field to see the ball. Or, to make the ball difficult to retrieve, a Creek conjurer would insert material from the corduroy, or "tie snake." Because that snake was thought to move by jumping or flipping, this would cause the ball to perform in the same manner. To obtain this magical snake substance, the medicine man sent an assistant to a cave where the snake had a nest; the assistant was given a special substance to quiet the snakes while he was stealing from their nest. Some medicine men hid a flea in a ball to make it "lively."

During a game, such a "doctored" ball had to be secretly substituted for the regular ball already in play. A special Creek "chief ball" containing inchworms would be snuck into a game after three goals had been scored, and in an 1852 string of Dakota matches, the losers of the first game won the second by switching to a special ball made years earlier by "an old war prophet." It is not known what abilities would be imparted to a doctored Menominee ball inside of which was hidden a sturgeon bone; the sturgeon is an important figure in the Menominee creation story, and the instruction to insert the bone had been received in a dream. Choctaw medicine men could create a "ball that would go straight" and a "medicine ball" with a long tail attached to it that supposedly made it hard for opponents to throw against the wind.

Finally, Indian lacrosse balls were given special handling and protection. After the Cherokee conjurer doctored the ball to be used in the game, he protected the ball overnight before the game by clamping it between the two pockets of the sticks of a center fighter. Marking the conclusion of the summer ceremonial cycle in the Creek Green Corn ceremony, the medicine man gives a special blessing to the two balls to be used. Previously they had been filled with herbal medicines by the town chief or "medicine-maker." After circling the ceremonial fire, holding the two balls tied together with a thong hanging from a short stick, the medicine man leads the two lines of players behind him away from the town square. Before heading for the field, they stop momentarily for call-and-response chanting, followed by a long, wailing cry from his assistant; this is answered by war whoops from the Creek players as they bang their sticks together.

What was the fate of a special ball after a game? After ritual games of the Mexican Kickapoo, they threw the balls far into the hills. If children should happen to retrieve them, they were allowed to play with them but only using sticks and only after all adoption ceremonies of the tribe had been concluded and the people moved into their summer houses.

CHEATING AND FOUL PLAY

The pale moon legend was told for its moral lesson against cheating or unfair play in lacrosse. But what exactly was considered unfair in the Indian game, and what constituted cheating? Unlike white teams, Indians did not play according to rules agreed upon by athletic organizations and published in manuals specifying infractions and penalties to be imposed.

Some tribes did have men who functioned as referees—Cherokee "drivers" or "stickmen," for instance, who wore turbans and carried long willow switches. (Elsewhere they wore neckties or hats with white feathers.) Because the game was characterized by its "no holds barred" action, tripping, holding, and slashing were not considered foul play (see plate 4), so the principal function of these "drivers" was to keep the game from slowing down, not inflicting penalties. They would break up a wrestling match between opponents if it was slowing down the action. The American artist George Catlin described the individual wrestling matches that broke out during Choctaw games: "Their stricks [*sic*] are dropped, and the parties are unmolested, whilst they are settling it between themselves."* If the stickman decided that they were fighting for too long, he could begin to switch them on their backs to get them to return to the game. Because the small hide southeastern ball was frequently and easily lost in the grass, their switches had another function—to point out where the ball was in case the players had lost track of it.

What exactly was "unfair play"? There are reports of "dirty players," but no specific examples are given of what their offensive behavior might have been. In Yuchi ceremonial games the chief clan opposed what one writer called the "mean Warriors." Did that describe them as dirty players? When Montrealer George Beers and his colleagues attempted to "civilize" the Mohawk game about 1850, he set out a list of violations, including throwing a stick at another player, holding, spearing with a stick, and verbally threatening another player. It is likely, however, that these sorts of behavior had crept into the white man's game and were not elements found in the Mohawk game that served as their model.

With so few rules in the Indian game, what real need was there for referees? Consider, for instance the "out-of-bounds" regulations of today's field game. There were no sidelines to most Indian fields, which the hapless Hobart team one time discovered in a game against Onondaga players. The ball carrier playing by Indian rules simply disappeared into the woods at one side of the field and reemerged from the trees near the end of the field to score the winning goal!

What about rules to judge whether a team had actually scored or not? There were no such things as crease violations, but one assumes there had to

*George Catlin, *Letters and Notes on the Manners, Customs, and Condition of the North American Indians,* 2 vols. (London: Tosswill and Myers, 1841; reprint, Minneapolis: Ross and Haines, 1965), 2:126.

be occasional disagreements over whether a team had scored properly. In the Great Lakes game, for instance, a player had to strike the single goalpost with the ball, either thrown or while still carried in the pocket of the stick. This rule applied even in some unusual practices of goal location. On the Lac Court Oreilles Ojibwe Reservation in northwestern Wisconsin, the single post was erected at the bottom of a 50-foot-wide pit, guarded by several play-ers. One still had to hit the post; if the ball missed it and went past a "foul line" (it is not clear where that was—possibly the far edge of the pit or beyond), the goal didn't count, and the ball would be returned to centerfield for another face-off. One can easily imagine controversy over accurate scoring in such an arrangement, but were there officials to make that determination?

Consider as well the cardinal rule against using the hand, which seems uni-versal in the game. In fact, the Cherokee word for a foul, *uwagi*, means liter-ally "with the hand." A player in trouble might deliberately pick up the ball with his hand to stop the game. In some places this rule applied to the feet as well; Iroquoian players once observed this rule, but it had disappeared by the mid-nineteenth century except for in Cayuga ritual games.

There were situations in which the hand rule did not apply. The Cherokee practiced considerable flexibility in observing the "no hands" infraction. A player was allowed to carry the ball in his hands if he picked it up with his sticks. Also, one could transfer a ball by hand to or from a teammate's stick; hand-to-hand transfers, however, were infractions, resulting in a foul and requiring a new face-off on the field where the foul took place. New regula-tions were later introduced in the Cherokee game; for example, by 1943, all players were required to play with sticks until someone had caught the ball in his hand and run to score with it. Also, after a Cherokee team had scored 11 points, its players could discard their sticks and play just with their hands, although their opponents needed to continue using sticks until they, too, had reached 11 goals.

A distinction should be made between game officials and scorekeepers, al-though the same person may have performed both functions. Indian score-keepers usually kept count by inserting sharpened pegs in the ground or mak-ing marks to keep track of the score; among the Alabama Indians of Texas, the scorekeeper drew a straight line in the earth, adding vertical strokes to either side to represent goals scored.

In the literature one finds an occasional mention of "officials," such as a person empowered to break a tie by extending the length of the game. By the twentieth century some lacrosse traditions had adopted specific rules about game length that seemed modeled after other sports of the dominant white culture. When Mississippi Choctaw games were revived, they began to be played on the high school football field; the game introduced four 12-minute periods, then moved into "sudden death" in case of a tie.

Playing with an Evil Head (Seneca)

In another Seneca legend collected by Curtin and Hewitt (see chapter 1), a transformed human head serves for a lacrosse ball. A woman's head, decapitated by a powerful cannibal, is kept alive by her children in the hollow of a tree, where they feed it scraps of meat from the cannibal's hunts. The head's insatiable appetite, however, causes it to escape and fly through the air in search of human food. Having reached one village, it starts devouring the people there.

> The old mothers now cautioned their children again to take great care and make no missteps. Now the youngest one thought of some bear's fat they had in the lodge, and the idea came to her that the only way they could kill the Head was by use of this. After the Head had eaten the first girl and was chasing the others through the lodge, the bear's oil began to boil. As they threw the boiling oil, it singed and burned the Head, killing it (the animated Head was merely the skull with long projecting teeth).
>
> All wishing to give thanks, the mothers said: "We ought to have a game of ball. Your brother is free. It is our duty to give thanks. The ball shall be this Head." Picking up the Head, she carried it out, calling in a loud voice, "Here, warriors! is a ball you can have to play with." Soon a great crowd of people came together with their netted clubs and began to play. All the players were wild beasts of the woods. The man stood near and saw the wild beasts playing ball with his wife's head. All tried to get the ball, and in this way they wore it out.
>
> The dog now came up to his master and told him that his wife was dead; and when it said: "Your wife is dead," his strength seemed to leave him; his arms dropped down, and he was sad. The invisible brother said: "You feel grieved; for my part I am glad I do not see why you should be sad; she would have devoured you if they had not killed her. Now there is

nothing to harm us. Your old uncle has gone back to his own home and will not trouble us now that he has eaten your wife's flesh." He added: "Your children are living in this direction (pointing westward)"; be of good courage, and go after them. I shall return. You will continue in one direction with your dogs until you reach the boys. You need never bear to suffer such hardships again." So saying, he went home, and when the brother looked after him he had disappeared.

Source: *J. Curtin and J. N. P. Hewitt, "Seneca Fiction, Legends, and Myths," in the* Twenty-eighth Annual Report of the Bureau of America Ethnology *(Washington, DC: Government Printing Office, 1911), 294–95.*

Just as its spherical shape is obviously behind its association with a lacrosse ball in the Cherokee legend of the pale moon, the roundness of the human head here and in other stories suggests that it might be used in place of the ball. There has even been speculation that lacrosse descended from some ancient sport in which heads taken in warfare were used as game balls.

An evil head in pursuit of victims is a theme in many North American legends. The human head, we shall see, plays a role in a Ho-Chunk (Winnebago) story about Red Horn, who as part of his lacrosse "uniform" wears earrings made of tiny human heads (chapter 4). These peculiar ornaments unnerve his opponents considerably; whenever the heads stick out their tongues and wink their eyes, the distraction causes them to fall apart from laughter.

The head is also equated with the bulbous end of a common war club, some of which were actually decorated with human facial features (figure 10). Usually the rounded object is depicted as in the clutches of some powerful bird, like the talons of an eagle. If not the claws of a bird of prey or a snake's mouth, then a human hand—in one case, at least. The butt of a handsome Cayuga stick made sometime before 1845 is carved to show a human hand clutching the ball—the cardinal violation in lacrosse. The belief surrounding the held ball is symbolic: when the warrior goes into battle with the war club, the bird releases the ball, which then flies to its intended victim to kill him.

It is significant in the story that the lacrosse players are warriors; the mother has invited them for the game she is sponsoring in thanksgiving for the death of the evil head. By giving them the head to use for a ball, it is as though it is a war trophy such as warriors brought back from the war path. With their lacrosse sticks, the warriors fight over the head, probably already

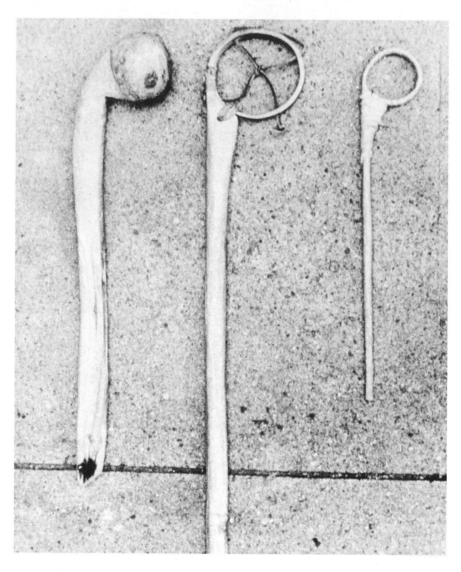

FIGURE 10.
Three Ojibwe artifacts in the author's collection. Note their close resemblance. From *left* to *right*: a war-club terminating in a ball from the Garden River Reserve (southeastern Ontario); a lacrosse stick made by Franklin Basina from the Red Cliff Reservation (northwestern Wisconsin); and a drumstick from the Bad River Reservation (20 miles south of Red Cliff in Wisconsin). All three objects are traditional items made in the mid-twentieth-century.

Photo courtesy of the author

burned beyond recognition, trying to gain possession. The violence of their contest is such that they "wear it out." Having one's head reduced to a game piece is, of course, demeaning enough. Here it symbolically represents a way of taunting so familiar in combat situations and later transferred to lacrosse competition or gloating in victory celebrations, such as when warriors proudly recounted their war deeds in dances, first striking the "war post" with their war club. Wearing out the head represents its ultimate destruction: having lost all its powers, it is no longer capable of pursuing and eating humans.

The First Lacrosse Ball (Menominee)

As in the Seneca legend, the close relationship between warfare and lacrosse figured in other stories and traditions. It was not by accident that Iroquois warriors were often chosen on the basis of their athletic skills as demonstrated in lacrosse, so that formerly many of the best lacrosse players came from the warriors' ranks.

Legendary explanations for the origins of lacrosse equipment seem to be prevalent in the Great Lakes area, as in a Menominee story collected by Frances Densmore from Mitchell Beaupre on his reservation in northeastern Wisconsin sometime in the early 1920s.

The Menominee Indians, or *amaceqtaw* ("the people who live with the seasons") in their own language, are the oldest continuous inhabitants of the state of Wisconsin and one of the few tribes east of the Mississippi River to still inhabit their ancestral lands. Their name was given them by their neighbors the Ojibwe in reference to the prevalence of wild rice in their diet (*Manoomin* is the Ojibwe word for wild rice). Their diet also included sturgeon and maple sugar. Once inhabiting 9 million acres reaching from Lake Michigan to the Mississippi, through land cessions they were gradually reduced to a Wisconsin county established in 1934. Possessing the largest single tract of timberland in the area, today the tribe relies on their timber resources and follows a rigorous policy of sustained development.

Traditionally, the Menominee were divided into various clans, each with a specific responsibility. They participated on the American side of the Black Hawk War of 1832, and in the Civil War a predominantly Menominee regiment fought on the side of the Union. Although in the mid-nineteenth century lumber barons maneuvered to acquire Menominee lands, the Indians were able to survive that pressure as well as the allotment system following the Dawes Act of 1887, which permitted individual owners to sell off their property. Their traditional material culture was similar to that of Algonquian-speaking neighbors, the Potawatomi and Ojibwe, with whom they shared the medicine lodge and the Big Drum ceremony.

Frances Densmore (1867–1957) was trained in "classical" music—the art music of Western Europe—but became interested in American Indian music when as a child she heard at night distant Sioux performances near the family home in Red Wing, Minnesota. In her career she went on to record more than 2,500 Edison wax cylinders of Indian music from more than 30 tribes. She used the recordings as a basis for studies of their music, published over a 50-year span as various bulletins of the Bureau of American Ethnology. Densmore began her study with Ojibwe singers on reservations in her home state; her first major publication, *Chippewa Music* (1910), is an early landmark publication in the discipline of ethnomusicology. Attending a ceremonial drum transfer of the Wisconsin Lac du Flambeau Ojibwe to the neighboring Menominee sparked her interest in Menominee music, ultimately leading her to publish the monograph that contains this legend.

A man named Ackinit (Uncooked) had a dream. In his dream he had been hunting in the woods all winter and had a great deal of game hanging up. As the spring approached and sap was flowing in the maple trees, it was time for sugar making, so he thought he might as well stay for the sugar camp. The snow was deep. One night there was a severe storm with thunder and rain. Everyone was frightened and could not lie down, and the wigwam was bright with lightning. Suddenly Ackinit heard a voice say, "Ackinit, go on top of the bluff where you killed the deer. We have left something there for you to show your friends every spring." Ackinit's oldest boy was about six years old and had never been in the deep woods with his father. Ackinit wanted to take his first child with him, so he told his wife about the voice that said, "Something has been left for you on top of the bluff where you killed two deer."

Ackinit and his son traveled about three miles, and then he asked the little boy, "Do you see that place? There is no snow up there. I brought you to carry what we find." The boy said, "What shall we look for?" His father replied, "Medicine."

When Ackinit and his son reached the top of the bluff they found a big nest full of feathers. They were out of breath when they reached the top, and Ackinit saw the feathers shaking like snow that is blown by the wind. He stepped softly because the motion looked as though something alive was in the nest. Looking in, he saw a green egg, and a voice said, "Keep this and show it to your people every spring." The little boy carried the egg back to the sugar camp.

This egg was left by the thunderers, who said, "We want tobacco. We live among the rocks, but your people have earth and can raise tobacco. Each person who comes to see this egg must give a little tobacco."

The next year, when they heard the first thunder, Ackinit called the people together and showed the egg. He collected tobacco and tossed it into the air for the thunderers and talked about his dream.

After Ackinit died, the egg was in the charge of his grandson, Wecananakwut, who kept it in his medicine bag and showed it every year. Mitchell Beaupre said he had seen it many times and that it was about the size of a duck's egg. It was in the feathers, which once were white but had become yellow with age. Wecananakwut collected a great heap of tobacco and passed it around, both men and women smoking while he talked about Ackinit and his dream. He said, "We will have a lacrosse game tomorrow, and if I'm telling the truth you will hear the thunderers coming to their game." The weather was clear when they began the game, but soon they could see a little cloud next to the horizon, and by the time they made a goal there was thunder and rain. Then Wecananakwut always said, "Don't be afraid. We gave tobacco to our grandfather yesterday and he has come to the game." (Beaupre said that Wecananakwut always said "grandfather," but he meant the thunderers.)

The informant said that the first lacrosse ball was made in imitation of the egg found by Ackinit in accordance with the instructions of the thunderers. The inside was of basswood twine, wound solid, and the outside was made of the hide of the black squirrel.

Source: *Frances Densmore*, Menominee Music, *Bulletin 102 of the Bureau of American Ethnology (Washington, DC: Government Printing Office, 1932), 36–37.*

Many Indian legends were told by elders to explain to children how certain unusual or important items in the culture came to be, why they were colored or shaped the way they were, and what purpose the item was meant to serve, particularly if the object had appeared in a dream. So it is scarcely surprising that the origin of lacrosse equipment should be explained in legends.

Those who played the sport were often struck by the resemblance of the sticks and the balls to other familiar items. Ball Club Lake on the Ojibwe Leech Lake Reservation in northern Minnesota, for example, was named after its shape—a long, narrow body of water (the stick) terminating in a large, bulbous-shaped bay (its pocket). It became the site of many of their *baga'a towe* (lacrosse) games whenever the waters receded to expose a large enough playing area for a lacrosse field. The similarity between the shapes of the traditional lacrosse stick and the war club makes these two "weapons" interchangeable in many Indian stories.

The legend explaining the discovery of the first lacrosse ball as a result of a dream shows the high regard the Menominee people had for their traditional sport. In relating the legend to Densmore, Beaupre, who had attended many of these ceremonies, stressed that the first Menominee lacrosse ball was made in imitation of the egg, following instructions from the thunderers (or Thunderbirds). In its construction, the inside of the ball was meant to have been of basswood twine, wound solid, then covered with the skin of a black squirrel.

This raises an interesting historical question. The ball described by Beaupre is quite different from the ball most commonly known to the Menominee. Like neighboring Algonquian peoples (Ojibwe, Fox, Potawatomi), the Menominee generally played with the typical round, wooden Great Lakes ball, slightly smaller than the cup on the end of the handle. A ball made from squirrel skin encompassing a soft interior of basswood bark strips would have been more typical of the early northeastern balls, such as Iroquoian peoples formerly used. Perhaps the legend suggests the Menominee, too, once played with a lightweight, skin-stuffed ball in place of the hard, heavy pine balls that survive today mostly in museum collections.

The Menominee attribute the origin of their lacrosse ball to directions from the supernatural spirits. Everything about the legend emphasizes the special nature of this piece of game equipment. It is found in a nearly inaccessible, high place located near the realm of the thunderers, who play their own version of the game amid lightning and thunder. When first seen by Ackinit and his son, the egg is in a natural setting, a nest, as though recently laid there. The pure white feathers surrounding it quiver, which makes Ackinit wonder if the object is perhaps alive and causes him "to step softly," as though in the presence of some mysterious and holy creature. Even before arriving on the bluff, Ackinit has some notion of the purpose of his arduous journey. When his son inquires what it is they should be looking for, his father replies,

"Medicine!"—the Indian term for sacred, powerful, supernatural substances of any sort.

In many world cultures, just like planting and harvesting, certain athletic contests were coordinated with the change in seasons. The Ackinit tale is a good Woodlands example, paralleling the economic cycle of the Menominee. The hero has hunted all winter and has plenty of game (venison) stored away. Spring is near, and though there is still snow on the ground, the warm days and cool nights have started the sap rising in the maple trees and his people are collecting and boiling down sap. It is in the sugarbush that we find Ackinit when he receives his dream. Although the story has him telling the people "next year," one assumes that the first thunder clap was heard probably not long after his return to camp. Implicit in the legend is that Ackinit was responsible for the creation of the ball and the first lacrosse game as well, sponsored to honor the Thunderbirds. As in all ritual Menominee games, a tobacco offering is tossed in the air to satisfy their legendary desire for this plant, which humans easily garden but is unavailable to them.

Like many tribes, the Menominee believe lacrosse to be mimed warfare, and games are sponsored by a person like Ackinit whose guardian spirits are the thunderers. Such a person possessed a war bundle—traditionally one of the most sacred items a man could own. The bundle would have a buckskin wrapping, and, like all war bundles, the specific meaning of its contents was known only to him. It is believed that the first Menominee war bundle contained miniature copies of a war club, a lacrosse stick, and ball. (Miniaturization signified that the owner had control over the activities represented by the small items.)

The presence of war club and lacrosse equipment together in the war bundles of some tribes demonstrates their close association in the culture. When the owner of a Menominee war bundle received a dream from the thunderers requiring him to sponsor a game in front of the gift pole on the east side of the field, he placed his war bundle on a mat. For the duration of the game, he opened its buckskin cover to reveal its contents publicly—the only time he would expose the sacred items contained in the wrapping. About 1920 David Amab, who related the legend of the first Menominee lacrosse ball, described his grandfather in such a sponsorship role, wearing his fur turban with an eagle feather upright at the rear of the headpiece. The center of the white skin wrapping of the war bundle was painted red, the color of war. The small lacrosse ball in it was painted half red. In the Fox legend of the origins of lacrosse, the spirit bringing in the game held a stick in one hand; in the other was a red buckskin-covered ball.

The Wisconsin Potawatomi, neighbors of the Menominee, also hold a strong association between warfare and lacrosse. One Potawatomi "men's business bundle" contained a miniature canoe, war club, and lacrosse stick. It is not known whether the early-nineteenth-century artist who painted the portrait of collector Giacomo Costantino Beltrami, an Italian explorer, was aware of the symbolism of the items in his representation of the man, standing in a birch-bark canoe around 1823 in Ojibwe country, somewhere near the headwaters of the Mississippi River. Lying alongside one another on the cedar floorboards of the canoe are a war club and lacrosse stick, and in the bow of the canoe a war drum is propped up. (These objects are today exhibited in a natural science museum in Bergamo, Italy.)

The Menominee also believed the thunderers dictated not only the shape of the ball, as in the legend, but that the lacrosse stick be modeled after the war club. In striking a tree with their lightning, they left black marks showing where the wood should be cut for making the lacrosse stick. They believed that in the game the supernaturals played in the thunderhead, the lightning representing their ball.

These Wisconsin Indians were not the only ones with a ritual game dedicated to the thunderers. The Cayuga in southeastern Ontario hold a special thunder ritual in spring and summer as a means of petitioning rain in a dry season. Tobacco is offered by being burned in an outdoor fire, and men must fast and use emetics in preparation for the game. Their belief in the seven Thunder Gods is highlighted in many details of the ritual game: each team has seven players, goals are measured to be seven paces wide, and the first to reach seven goals wins.

3

WAGERS AND WARRIORS

Two recurrent themes in these legends are the practice of betting on games and the representation of players as warriors. The equation of the game with an actual battle, in which players lose their lives, is an old one in Indian lacrosse communities. Another Seneca story published by Curtin and Hewitt (see chapter 1) associates the ball with the head of a victim who has lost through wagering, just as in "Playing with an Evil Head" (chapter 2).

Playing for Heads (Seneca)

There was a very poor little old woman, who lived in the woods. She was so destitute that she was nothing but skin and bones. She dwelt in a smoky little lodge and cried all the time, both day and night. Her robe of skins was so old and dirty that one could not tell without difficulty of what material it was made. She had seven daughters, six of whom were carried off one after another by hostile people, while the seventh died.

The daughter who died had been buried some time when one night the old woman heard crying at the grave. Going to the grave with a torch, she found there a naked baby. The child had crawled up out of the grave through a hole in the earth. Wrapping the baby in her blanket, the old woman took it home. She did not know, she did not even suspect, that her daughter was with child when she died.

The little boy grew very rapidly. When he was of good size the old woman came home one day from gathering wood but could not find him. That night it stormed, with thunder and lightning raging. In the morning the child returned to her. His grandmother asked, "Where have you been, my grandson?" "Grandmother," said he, "I have been with my father; he took me to his home." "Who is your father?" "Hinon is my father; he took me home first, then we came back and were all about here last night." The old woman asked, "Was my daughter, your mother, in the grave?" "Yes," said the boy, "and Hinon used to come to see my mother." The old woman believed what he said.

As the boy grew up he used to make a noise like that of thunder, and whenever Hinon [the personification of thunder] came to the neighborhood he would go out and thunder, thus helping his father, for he was Hinon Hohawaqk, the son of Hinon.

Some time after this the boy asked his grandmother where his six aunts were, and the grandmother answered: "There are an old woman and her son, whose lodge is far away; they live by playing dice and betting. Your aunts went one by one with a company of people, and played dice (plum pits); being beaten, their heads were cut off. Many men and women have gone to the same place and have lost their heads." Hinon Hohawaqk answered, "I will go, too, and will kill that woman and her son." The old woman tried to keep him home, but he would not remain with her. He told her to make two pairs of moccasins for him. He was very ragged and dirty, so she made the moccasins and got him the skin of a flying-squirrel for a pouch.

Setting off toward the west, soon he came to a great opening where there was a large bark lodge with a pole in front of it, and on the pole a skin robe. He saw boys playing ball in the opening, and going on a side path he heard a great noise. After a while the people saw him, whereupon one of them said, "I do not know where that boy comes from." The old people were betting on the boys who were playing ball. Soon an old man came up to Hinon Hohawaqk and gave him a club; he played so well that the old man came again, saying, "We want you to play dice; all the people will bet on you." A bowl was placed on an elk skin lying under the pole. The woman and her son were there and the other people stood around. Hinon Hohawaqk answered, "I do not know how to play the game." The old man replied, "We will risk our heads on you"; so he followed the old man. He saw a white stone bowl as smooth as glass. The old woman was sitting there on the elk skin, ready to play, and Hinon Hohawaqk knelt down beside the bowl. She said, "You play first." "No," answered he, "you play first." So she took out her dice, which were round and made from plum stones, and blowing on them, cast them into the bowl, which she shook, at the same time calling out, "Game! Game!" The dice flew up into the air, all becoming crows and cawing as they went out of sight. After a while they came down, still cawing, and resumed the form of plum stones as they settled in the bowl.

The old woman had three plays to make a count of 17. She threw three times but got nothing. Then Hinon Hohawaqk in order to win took dice out of his pouch of flying-squirrel skin. The old woman wanted him to use her dice, but he would not touch them. Placing his dice in the bowl, he shook, whereupon the dice, becoming ducks, flew upward. They went very high, and all the people heard them as they rose; when they touched the bowl again they were plum stones, and scored 10. Then Hinon Hohawaqk shook the bowl again, calling, "Game! game!" while the old woman called out, "No game!" Back came the dice, scoring another 10. He cast the third time and scored 10 more. He had won. Then he called the people to see him cut off the heads of the old woman and her son.

"No," said the old woman, "you must play again. Here is my son; you must play ball with him, and if he loses we shall both forfeit our heads." At this Hinon Hohawaqk asked the old man what he thought. The people, seeing how skillful he was, said "Play!" Whereupon he went to the ball-ground, ragged and looking poor. There were but two playing, one on each side. Hinon Hohawaqk jumped, knocking the club far out of his opponent's hand. Then the old woman's son ran for his club, but before he could get it back Hinon Hohawaqk had sent the ball through the goal posts. This was repeated seven times and Hinon Hohawaqk won the game. "Now," said he to all the people, "you can have the heads of the old woman and her son." The two heads were cut off, and the boys played with the old woman's head over the whole field.

Source: *J. Curtin and J. N. P. Hewitt, "Seneca Fiction, Legends, and Myths," in the* Twenty-eighth Annual Report of the Bureau of America Ethnology *(Washington, DC: Government Printing Office, 1911), 372–74.*

This legend stresses the incremental nature of wagering on games. The betting in the story begins with a dice game—another form of gambling traditionally popular with Indians. There is subtle symbolism throughout this story. The old woman, who has killed Hinon Hohawaqk's six aunts when they had bet on dice games, is the obvious villain. Her plum stones magically turn into crows, whose very blackness is a harbinger of evil and death. By contrast, the hero's stones become harmless ducks. It is not known if the Seneca storyteller was familiar with the legend of the great game between the birds and the land animals (chapter 1), but there is a suggestion of that tale in the flying squirrel skin the grandmother uses to sew a pouch. Together with the bat, it will be recalled, the flying squirrel was created especially for the birds' side to help them win. They, too, used its skin, stretching it to provide him with flying power. The hero of this story keeps his plum stones in a flying squirrel pouch. The skin pouch probably represents a medicine bag, something in which every conjurer or medicine man kept whatever paraphernalia he used in demonstrating supernatural powers—here, plum stones that can turn into ducks and win at every toss. The evil woman and Hinon Hohawaqk possess nearly equal powers—turning dice into birds—but the hero's "medicine" is clearly stronger.

Betting incrementally reflects the old woman's desperation. Indians wagered great amounts on lacrosse games. Before a Cherokee game in 1834, the respective chiefs of the Hickory Log and Conawatee communities bet $1,000 each, which for impoverished North Carolina Indians at the time was a small fortune. Records show that the amount bet on a Georgia Cherokee game in 1823 amounted to $3,500. Missionaries and government agents were appalled that Indians squandered funds in such a sinful and wasteful manner.

A string of lacrosse games between bands of eastern Dakota in 1852 provides a good example of the incremental impetus of betting; the losses kept the competition going for several days. Players from Little Six's band opposed players from bands of Good Road, Gray Iron, and Sky Man. The white editor of *The Dakota Friend*, an Indian benevolent journal, documented the game in his publication, hoping to demonstrate the terrible impoverishing effect the games and betting on them were having on the already destitute Indians. The total amount wagered in the first game was $1,600. This was followed by several victories by Little Six's team totaling $2,600. The losers became winners and "upped the ante," adding a barrel of pork, two kegs of lard, and ten sacks of corn. By the editor's calculations, at the end of three days, a grand total of $4,600 had been spent—a hefty sum in central Minnesota territory in pioneer days. He concluded his account by asking imploringly, "How can Dakotas be otherwise than poor?"

Ojibwe George Tyosh remembered that lacrosse games played in the spring on the Lac Court Oreilles Reservation in northwestern Wisconsin would last as long as people had anything to bet; when they ran out of money, they would begin to wager their family's heirloom beadwork and clothing. When territorial disputes were settled by a lacrosse game, it was in the spirit of betting— the Cherokee won a huge tract of land in present-day Georgia from the Creek. Later, the Creek won a large beaver pond from the Choctaw in the early 1700s in present-day Noxubee County, Mississippi.

Wagering among the Eastern Cherokee was a serious component of their lacrosse games. When one team challenged another, all details of the contest had to be agreed upon by both parties or the game would be called off. The pace and amount of betting were directly affected. They distinguished between "a big game," which meant one with veteran players on both teams and understandably high-stakes betting, and smaller, less important games, with amateur players and consequently considerably less wagering. Rematches were almost always scheduled. Any team refusing challenges several times was obliged to challenge the loser to give them a chance to recoup losses. In the interest of general tribal peacefulness, to even things up each spring the Cherokee would "wipe the slate clean," ignoring former wins and losses.

In the 1890s an irate Mississippi citizen, H. S. Halbert, described the game of lacrosse as immoral: "The greatest obstacle in the way of the educational and religious progress [of the Mississippi Choctaw]. To put it mildly, the ball play is the most demoralizing institution in Mississippi. It is, in a great measure, now-a-days manipulated or controlled by a white swashbuckler element, and gambling, whiskey drinking, fighting, and not infrequently bloodshed have become the regular concomitants of the play."* Halbert's concerns were addressed when the state of Mississippi in 1898 outlawed gambling on Indian lacrosse games along with cockfights and dueling.

Gambling on Indian lacrosse games, although an old practice, was a frequently cited evil that eventually in some places contributed to the decline,

---

*Cited in John R. Swanton, "Source Material for the Social and Ceremonial Life of the Choctaw Indians," *Bureau of American Ethnology Bulletin Number 103* (Washington, DC: Government Printing Office, 1931), 24–25.

and even the disappearance, of the Indian sport. Betting among the Cherokee gradually tapered off—at least in the size and value of the items being
wagered. In 1828, in an attempt to make the North Carolina Cherokee more
"civilized," the government eliminated many of their amusements with the
exception of "the manly play of ball." However, one could no longer wager
property as previously, except for trifling items, such as an article of clothing.
The act of wagering was so commonplace that the subject was reflected in
many aspects of Cherokee traditional culture, including music. A song performed by women during the traditional ball game dance held the night before a game told of anticipated winnings: "What a fine horse I shall win. I'm
going to win 'a pretty one.'" Even today, although gambling on games is no
longer allowed, older, conservative Cherokee who recall former times might
still make small bets among themselves. After a 1958 game, anthropologist
Raymond Fogelson asked a friend, Molly Sequoyah, how she had liked the
game. "She responded with a sly wink, displaying a new handkerchief she had
just won."*

Although the specific reasons are not recorded, government authorities
canceled an Ojibwe game at annuity payments on Madeline Island in 1855.
With so many visiting Indians in attendance and so much fresh cash in their
hands, the government probably feared a lacrosse competition between Lake
Superior players and visiting inland Ojibwe would have prompted considerable betting. The practice almost always occurred whenever games were held
at some large government-sponsored event, such as annuity payments or
peace treaty signings. It was a peace treaty meeting that provided artist
George Catlin the opportunity to observe Dakota-Ojibwe games at Fort
Snelling (present-day Minneapolis), where he painted portraits of the players and recorded a description the game.

TEAMS

In "Playing for Heads," the lacrosse game is only between Hinon Hohawaqk
and the wicked woman's son in a one-on-one battle. Lacrosse legends in
mythical time often result from some hero being challenged to demonstrate
his power or bravery—frequently as the first (or more often the last) in a

---

*Raymond Fogelson, "The Cherokee Ballgame: A Study in Southeastern Ethnology" (Ph.D.
diss., University of Pennsylvania, 1962), 184–85.

string of challenges. Probably each player in this one-on-one game symbolically represents a side or a team, and the progress of the game and outcome are what are important, not how many were on the field.

The details of the game itself conform to what we know of Indian lacrosse: Hinon Hohawaqk is able to knock the son's stick from his hands, and before his opponent can recover it, the hero scores by throwing the ball between the goalposts, just as formerly one used to score in the Seneca game. He wins with seven goals, a ritual number still played to win in certain Iroquoian ceremonial games.

There is little question that many games in the distant past had large numbers of players. Gradually, it seems these teams were reduced to more manageable sizes. Some historical accounts may exaggerate. An account of a seventeenth-century exhibition game of the Miami Indians claimed 2,000 warriors took part. This number may simply have represented a deliberate "show of force" to impress the new French Indian agent. Moreover, the report really only states that 2,000 showed up with sticks, not that that many actually played. Another exaggerated account is George Catlin's figure of 200 Choctaw players at Fort Gibson (Indian Territory) in 1834. Contemporaneous reports on Choctaw lacrosse of that period give no more than 50 as the largest number of players. No doubt Catlin's paintings of the game were intended to convey the great excitement of the sport, and the more figures he could crowd onto the canvas, the greater would be the effect of a congested battle on the viewer. (Often Catlin painted for effect, taking liberties with accuracy.)

The social context surrounding any game and where it took place were also important. Many games were put on to impress visiting VIPs—exactly Catlin's reception at Fort Snelling in 1835. The Indian agent, Lawrence Taliaferro, in advance had told the Indians that Catlin was "a great medicine man," who had seen games of other tribes and wished to see if the Ojibwe and Dakota were as talented. The agent also promised the Indians a 21-gun salute, and Catlin sweetened the deal with a pledge of barrels of pork, flour, and tobacco. With such incentives, it is little wonder every Indian who could play would rush to get into this specially staged game. It lasted two hours, before the Indians departed to the agency to demonstrate tribal dances for their important guest. That formula of a lacrosse game followed by native "war dances" performed by the players would be repeated in the nineteenth century. When Canadians toured Indian teams in Europe, posters advertising the event never failed to point out that spectators would get doubly entertained for their attendance.

Another exhibition game staged for "an important person" was a Cherokee game in 1797 at Tellico, Tennessee, in which 600 are said to have played—a figure ten times the highest number ever recorded for a Cherokee game. In fact, when James Mooney conducted his North Carolina fieldwork around 1880 there were only 9 to 12 per side, and 22 was the largest number any of his consultants could remember on a team. The 1797 Tellico game, put on for the visiting Duc de Orleans, later King of France, also offered rewards for players: 6 gallons of brandy to the winners. So important was the event that the French visitors were accompanied to the game field with pomp, provided by the garrison's drummers.

Hearsay reports tend to become exaggerated with time, too. In his published account of a game played between the Seneca and Mohawk, also in 1797, William Stone states, "the combatants numbered about 600 upon a side." A later paragraph, however, explains that 600 were prepared to play. Actually only 60 per side played at one time, and these were rotated every 15 or 20 minutes, until all had had a chance to participate in this important face-off between the two Iroquois nations.

Wakayabide Is Killed Playing Lacrosse and Later Takes Revenge (Ojibwe)

Like other stories, this Ojibwe legend focuses on aspects of warfare. It was collected in 1944 by Victor Barnouw from Sam Whitefeather, a Lac du Flambeau Ojibwe. The image of lightning occurs several times relating it to battle. In the previous tale, Hinon Hohawaqk was the son of the personification of Thunder; here, whenever the chief picks up or takes down his war club, lightning bolts shoot from it. Once again, the danger and potential of death resulting from playing lacrosse is central to the story. The hero, Wakayabide, is enticed into playing against the advice of his wife. The legend provides another example where a supernatural dog appears to save the day, just as in "A Dog's Power Beats the Old Chief" (chapter 1). Animals again play in the game, but here they are two species of bears.

Probably the most widely dispersed Indian people of North America, the Ojibwe (*anishinaabeg*, "original people") are found today spread out from southeastern Ontario throughout the upper Great Lakes areas and westward as far as Montana and Saskatchewan. Two-thirds of the estimated 200,000 Ojibwe live in Canada, and about 10 percent are fluent in one of the three or four dialects of the language. (Their name was corrupted to Chippewa by nonnatives.) Their migration story places their people as originating on the eastern shore of North America and following a long journey westward through the Great Lakes. They carried on sporadic military encounters with their traditional enemies, the Fox and Dakota, well into the nineteenth century. The Ojibwe subsisted traditionally on maple sugar, wild rice, fish, and venison, and many of their traditional crafts made use of the white birch. They were recognized as probably the most skilled of the birch-bark canoe builders.

When Victor Barnouw was a graduate student in the doctoral program in anthropology at Columbia, he joined a research team directed by Robert Ritzhenthaler, the head of the Anthropology Section of the Milwaukee Public Museum. The team was sent to northern Wisconsin to collect ethnological data and interview Ojibwe living on the Lac Court Oreilles and Lac du Flambeau Reservations in 1941, 1942, and 1944. Barnouw was particularly interested in mythology and was given this tale from Sam Whitefeather at Lac du Flambeau. Barnouw later went on to teach anthropology at the University of Wisconsin-Milwaukee.

Down the hill there was a village with all kinds of wigwams. One of them was pretty long; it must have been a *midewigan,* a Medicine Dance lodge. Pretty soon an old lady came out of the long wigwam and came running up to the fire. She didn't expect to see anyone there, but then she saw Wakayabide and could see his guts in plain sight. She saw his teeth too. She was scared and ran back down the hill and jumped into her wigwam. She nudged her old man. "I've seen a *manido* [spirit] by the fire. His guts and teeth are in plain sight; he's naked."

The old man, who was the chief, said, "Look over there. There's a stranger by the woodpile."

His son, a clever boy, jumped up and said, "Well, well. It can't be someone wishing to become my brother-in-law."

Some other older fellows said, "Here, here, young man; don't talk that way! That's a *manido.* If you talk like that, he'll come and kill us some day. Be careful. A *manido* has come to us, so we'd better be good to him."

Some kids foolishly said, "I wouldn't say he was a *manido*. His guts are in plain sight."

The old man said, "Be good to that man! Don't talk like that!"

The young man of the lodge had three sisters. He was the young chief, Madjikiwis. He said, "I'm going to go and take a look at my future brother-in-law." He took up his [war] club. It had a big ball at the end of it; when he picked it up, sparks flew all over the room. That's how powerful he was. There was thunder and lightning.

He went up to Wakayabide and said, "My friend, I want you to have a new home. When we go into the wigwam, go to my sisters. There's a heavy-set woman; that's one of them. The next one is a medium-sized woman. The next is a smaller one. I'll give you the smallest. I want you to be my brother-in-law. Pay no attention to what people say about them. When you get to the first one, the fat one, she will say, 'Stop here and sit down; I'm the one you're going to marry.' Just keep right on going. The next one will say the same thing. She'll want you to sit next to her. But keep right on going to the smallest one. That's the sister I want you to marry. All right, get up and follow me."

He got up. People all came and stared at them. One little kid shouted, "Do you call him a *manido* with his guts and teeth in plain sight? I wouldn't call him *manido*."

An elder present said, "Here, here. You be quiet. The *manido* will fix you after a while, if you talk like that."

When they came to the doorway, the young chief went to his place, and Wakayabide turned the way he'd been told to go. The man came to the big fat woman, who said, "Sit down here, that's where you're supposed to sit," but he kept right on going. The second one said, "So you've come to me now. Sit right here with me." He kept on until he came to a little tiny woman. She said nothing, and he sat right down.

He looked around at all the things that Madjikiwis owned, hanging up from the lodge poles. When his new brother-in-law hung up his war club, Wakayabide saw the sparks fly out.

His new wife started to inform him: "We have all kinds of games here. I want you to be careful. The people here are dangerous. They kill each other. You won't live very long if you play in any of their games."

The three sisters were having affairs with some men, powerful men. Everybody heard that Madjikiwis had a new brother-in-law, so they all wanted to see him. The first man, a great big tall man, came in and

announced, "I've come to see my brother." There was a great big rock
inside the wigwam. This man came and sat on the rock. He was carrying
a big tobacco pouch. He talked to Wakayabide: "I'm glad you've come;
I'm glad to see you. We have a lot of fun here, lots of games. We'd like
you to play with us." Then he said, "Now I'm going to show you my
power." He picked up the big rock—solid rock—and tossed it up and
down. He walked over to Wakayabide, playing with the rock to scare
him. He almost dropped it. Then he set it down and said, "That's my
power. That's the kind of man I'd be if I stayed with that woman," he
boasted.

Wakayabide filled up his pipe with tobacco. Then he tightened the
cord of his bow. He had to get his revenge on the insolent braggard. This
man was naked, so Wakayabide was going to shoot him between the
legs. He wasn't going to hurt him, just graze him. He pulled the bow, and
the arrow just grazed him. The man took his tobacco and ran outside.
Outside you could hear him laughing: "Ha, ha, ha! I've found a man
who's better than I am. I give up! He's a *manido,* so I won't bother him
anymore."

The next day another man came to see him. (Because the first man
that had come was a grizzly bear and this one was a polar bear, Wakayabide realized that those people had the power to change into animals.)
This man said, "I've come to see my brother." He had a tobacco pouch
and a long pipe too. He sat on the big rock there. He said, "I've got to
show you my power." As he scratched the stone, flames began springing
out of it, and rocks flew around, but it didn't bother those people. They
just sat there. Then he said, "That's how I'd be if I knew I'd have that
woman," sitting down to fill up his pipe.

Wakayabide got his bow and arrows out and shot this man by the
head, just shaved his skull. Then that man jumped up and ran out. Outside he laughed: "My brother is a better man than I am. I'll give up,
and I won't bother him anymore."

There was one more visitor, who came the next day: a human being
this time, a well-built fellow. His wife knew about what would happen
and told Wakayabide: "The men that go [have sex] with me are going to
try out your power. Be careful. Say nothing to anybody."

This man came in. When he raised the curtain of the wigwam, a flood
of water came in—red clay water. That's the power he had. The current
was strong. Wakayabide was just about to float away, when his little wife

grabbed him and tied him with a sash and held him. He could hardly get his breath. He was near drowning when the water went down, but it dried in no time. The other people in there didn't even feel it. They just sat there. It was nothing to them. Then the man sat on the rock, filled up his pipe, and said, "That's the kind of man I'd be if I married this woman."

Wakayabide got out his bow and arrows again. This time he shot the rock right in the center. He thought to himself, "A little piece of rock will be in that man's body," and that's what happened. That man said, "I can't beat that man! He's too good for me. I give up!"

So, now three men had tried to drive Wakayabide out, but they couldn't because he had too much power.

The next day, early in the morning, there was an announcer going around the circle of wigwams in the village. He announced: "Today we have a lacrosse game. Madjikiwis's new brother-in-law must play, too."

Wakayabide's wife said, "Be careful! I don't want you to go. They'll kill you."

The man laughed. "They can't kill me. I'll go and look on, anyway. If I don't play, I'll just look on."

Madjikiwis was losing the game all the time. He lost all of his clothing. He wanted his brother-in-law to play for him, which is what he had intended before, although he hadn't told Wakayabide.

Everybody was out in the field. Wakayabide stood with his bow and arrow, watching. Pretty soon one of the fellows, the grizzly bear, came over to him. "Here, brother." He gave him a lacrosse stick.

"I don't know how to play. I can't play," said Wakayabide.

"No, no, you must play," replied the bear.

"All right, I'll try," said Wakayabide, as he took the lacrosse stick.

Wakayabide had left his belt behind in the wigwam, so his protective spirit, the wolf, wasn't there. Out in the woods the wolf had told him never to leave the belt and always take it along.

The ball was headed towards Wakayabide. His teammate said, "Grab the ball and run with it!"

He grabbed the ball with his club and ran for the goal. The other man followed. Instead of taking the ball away, the bear jumped on his bare back and tore his skin to the bone. Wakayabide dropped dead right there. Alas, when the game was over, there was no Wakayabide coming home. They must have cut him up into pieces and shared the meat, thought his little wife.

The woman was worrying about him. She asked people where he was, but they didn't tell her. That night all the families feasted on the meat. Wakayabide's wife was so worried she couldn't sleep. The wolf hidden inside the belt realized something was wrong with his master, so he started to howl inside the belt. The woman heard that noise. She kept quiet and listened. It sounded like a wolf howling. At first, it was like a wolf way off in the woods. Then she noticed that it was coming from the belt. She found a little pocket there. She opened it and found a tiny dog. She set it on the ground. She knew right away that it belonged to Wakayabide.

The dog shook, like all dogs do when wet, and began to grow. Then he dashed outside right away. He ran all over town. He assembled all Wakayabide's bones and put them together in the shape of a man. There was one joint he couldn't find—the elbow. He ran all over but couldn't find it. Then he saw smoke going up out in the woods. There was a young woman living by herself out in the woods in a seclusion hut because she was menstruating. She had a piece of meat too—the elbow joint. The dog ran over there. The woman had the bone he was looking for. He sat by the doorway, looking at the woman, wishing for her to throw the bone down. She chewed and kept saying, "My, my! That tastes good. I can't stop chewing." She saw the dog and said, "I guess he wants that bone. I won't give it to him, though, it tastes too good." The dog moved a little nearer, but she commanded, "Go outside! I want that bone myself."

The dog got tired of waiting, so he jumped at her, grabbed the bone, and dashed off. Now he had all the bones. Then he hollered. The bones lumped together in the shape of a man. He hollered again. Flesh formed on the bones. He hollered again. Then Wakayabide's eyes opened up.

The people were surprised to hear that dog holler. The elder, who had been trying to make the young people behave, said, "I wouldn't be surprised if that man is coming alive again."

When the wolf hollered the fourth time, Wakayabide's breath began to return to him. The wolf said, "You didn't listen to me, my grandchild, so I came to save you. That's what happens when you don't listen. Get up now. We'll go home." The hero's wife was glad to see him again. She said, "I found that little dog in your belt. He's saved your life. Always take your belt along with you now."

The next day the announcer went around again. "Today we have another lacrosse game. Madjikiwis's brother-in-law ought to play too."

His wife said to him, "Don't go. They'll kill you again."

He said, "No, I want to go." He wanted to get his revenge on that fellow who had killed him.

That morning he put on his belt and went out. He was looking for the man he'd played against the day before. "Hey, brother," he said, "come here. I want to play with you."

The bear said, "Oh, sure!"

The ball was tossed up. The bear said, "I'll show you how to play!" He took the ball, but Wakayabide pursued him with two arrows in his hands. Wakayabide jumped on the bear with his two arrows and buried them in his skin. He tore the bear to pieces with the arrows and killed him. Then he walked away. They used to play for a live person. That's how they got their food, their meat. They ate each other. The other people cut up the bear and cooked him. They passed the meat around to all the families. Wakayabide had some of it too. It tasted good, nice and fat.

But the bear came alive again the next day, too. He was a powerful man.

Source: *Victor Barnouw,* Wisconsin Chippewa Myths and Tales *(Madison: University of Wisconsin Press, 1977), 142–48; for other versions, see Henry Schoolcraft,* The Indian in His Wigwam *(New York: W. H. Graham, 1848), 106, and Walter James Hoffman, "The Menomini Indians," in* Fourteenth Annual Report of the Bureau of American Ethnology, 1892–1893 *(Washington, DC: Government Printing Office, 1897), 182–96.*

Many threads run through this unusual lengthy tale, among which are displays of supernatural power and strength, cannibalism, the protection of one's guardian spirit—especially a dog—and the consequences of ignoring the spirit. When a stranger, Wakayabide, turns up in an Indian village (the presence of a "long medicine wigwam" identifies it as Ojibwe, or at very least somewhere in the western Great Lakes area), there is initial disagreement over who or what he might be. The elders are suspicious that Wakayabide might be a spirit (*manido*) because, although he is naked, his teeth and guts are visible, as though through an x-ray. When young kids poke fun at the idea that Wakayabide is a spirit, they are warned to be careful in their remarks, lest the spirit return and "fix" (punish, or get even with) them.

Like many traditional legends, this one is filled with symbolism, much of it erotic. Freudian folklore analysts would insist on interpreting the sexual symbolism here—the phallic connotations of the deadly arrows and elbow joint that the menstruating woman refuses to surrender, shooting the grizzly bear between the legs. Consistent with the violence throughout the tale is the color red, the color of war: the near drowning of the hero in red clay water, the blood of the menstruating woman.

But what does the legend tell us about lacrosse? The story is really about risking death by playing the game. Several themes from other legends are also touched on here. Madjikiwis is "losing the game all the time" and is down to his bare skin. This fits with what we know about the wagering on Indian lacrosse games, which even the players indulged in. When in desperation over losses, a person (or team) would "up the ante," challenging the winners to more games to recoup their earlier losses. This happens here when, to get even or take revenge, the spirit proposes another game with the bear that had killed him.

Violence and death are the leading themes here, symbolizing the extremes people went to in their wagers, at times putting up a wife and children or their own services to a winner. The point is simply that the game is potentially injurious and could even result in death. Although Indian games were generally played peaceably and enjoyed as sport, the images of battle and warfare are plentiful in traditional American Indian lacrosse. They show up in game terminology, color associations, the symbolism of game equipment, and players' attitudes and ritual preparations.

In his analysis of the Cherokee ballgame, anthropologist Raymond Fogelson sees the termination of Cherokee warfare by the end of the eighteenth century as a turning point in the development of the lacrosse game. After that, young men needed a new outlet to vent their aggressive tendencies, which were formerly directed in battle against whites and other tribes. The prestige and status a man previously had earned as a warrior were now transferred to his performance in lacrosse—a new "field of battle."

Former players from many tribes felt that the federal government in ending warfare had weakened the manly virtues of their people. Knowing he would have a sympathetic ear, the Ho-Chunk (Winnebago) chief Little Priest complained to a visiting Indian from some western tribe, "One of our favorite games is the game of war. There was a time when we were a numerous people. Before our brother the white man came, I used to like to play that game against those of other tribes, but I never found any *men* to play with. All others of other Indian tribes used to call me elder brother. Because I was among all the greatest warriors. Since our friends the white man came, I have refrained from fighting. Things have changed now. We can no longer play that game."* Older players among the Choctaw around 1950 insisted that the current game had lost its energy of former times, when it was a man's game. They complained that younger players of the day were simply unable to take the punishment of the earlier game.

There was interchangeability of warfare and game terminology especially among southeastern tribes. In some languages there is an explicit interchange between the word for lacrosse and words for warfare, such as the Creek *hotti icos* (younger brother of war) or the Cherokee *da-na-wah-uwsdi* (little war).

Red—the color of war and blood—makes its way into the story in the red clay deluge that nearly drowns the hero. The association of red with the color of life-nurturing blood is as universal as it is with danger. Here Wakayabide nearly drowns when the third suitor causes his wigwam to flood. His new wife, who repeatedly cautions him against playing lacrosse, saves him by tying him with a sash. The salvation sash has its parallel in the belt containing his guardian spirit, the dog. Wakayabide foolishly neglects to wear the belt in the lacrosse game, thereby enabling his opponents to do him injury.

The magic belt is a form of supernatural protection, and the lesson to the hero is that such things are not to be taken lightly. Because Wakayabide forgets to wear his belt, he is deprived of its protection, thus vulnerable to injury and death. American Indian lacrosse players would understand its significance: one must never neglect the important preliminary steps before playing, that is, working with the team medicine man in performing the proper rituals for cleansing and empowering players.

The color red permeated traditional Indian lacrosse, especially among southeastern tribes. Red was applied to lacrosse sticks, and players' bodies were painted in red designs using vermilion—a valuable item in the traders' inventories. The Yuchi specialist making balls sewed together the soft deerskin covering of a lacrosse ball to conceal a smaller ball inside; it was made from red cloth and had been conjured. The lacrosse sticks were painted red and hung on the scaffold in the ball-game dance overnight before the game. Cherokee "sacred painters" prepared special red feathers formerly worn on

*Will C. McKern Papers, s.v. "Wisconsin notes," Anthropology Section, Milwaukee Public Museum.

the war path, later in lacrosse games. The assistant of the medicine man would tie them into players' hair and paint their faces red. Cherokee conjurers had protective formulas to recite to invoke the powers of the Red Hawk or Red Rattlesnake. The medicine man attached to any war party on each of four consecutive nights would recite the ritual formula, "What those who have been to war did to help themselves." The text began, *"hayi, yu!* Listen! Now instantly we have lifted up the red war club. Quickly his soul shall be without motion. There under the earth, where the black war clubs will be moving about like ball-sticks in the game, there his soul shall be, never to reappear."* (Just as red was associated with war, winning, and success, black was the color of death, failure, and losing—the color of the evil woman's crows in the previous legend, "Playing for Heads," perhaps foretelling that she would ulti- mately lose.)

Because men on the war path had been exposed to danger, injury, and death, they were considered to be in a "red condition" until released through special rituals. Because red represents danger, it explains why there were ta- boos about contact with menstruating women. In fact, women were prohib- ited from touching the game equipment because they might be experiencing their period. The fear was that menstrual blood was powerful and could weaken or destroy the inherent strength of a lacrosse stick or prevent the player from using it with any success in a game. (The destructive power of menstrual blood was reflected in many Indian attitudes. The Ojibwe, for ex- ample, would attribute the failure of a wild rice crop to a menstruating woman having bathed prior to the harvest in the lake or river where the rice grew.)

Once real fighting had ceased, many Cherokee warfare practices were con- tinued on into the lacrosse game. The cleansing preparations and sexual abstinence for three days prior to the war party's departure and the team's march to the ball field were identical to warpath practices. In both instances the conjurer mapped out the direction of the path taken by enemy combat- ants or lacrosse opponents and sent out scouts to search out enemy "spies." The scouts were needed to make certain the path was clear—in lacrosse in case the opposite team might have spilled "rabbit soup" on the path or other

---

*James Mooney, "The Sacred Formulas of the Cherokee," *Seventh Annual Report of the Bureau of America Ethnology, 1885–86* (Washington, DC: Government Printing Office, 1891), 388–89.

magical substances that would weaken players coming in contact with them. Both in warfare and game preparations, the men were marched single file and retired for four ritual "stopping places."

During the preparatory ball game dance, players would brandish their lacrosse sticks as though they were weapons. At one Creek ball game dance observed by anthropologist John Swanton, the ball to be played with was tied to a twig and inserted in the ground. Its end pointed in the direction of the opponents' community—as Swanton described it, "much as cannon are trained on an enemy."*

When warriors returned from battle they were considered to be "in a red condition," requiring purification; they were not free to join society until they were "cleansed." This required that they be sequestered in the town house for a period of fasting, bathing, and taking emetics (purgatives to induce vomiting). Similarly, rather than intermingling with the crowd of spectators, Cherokee lacrosse players were directly "taken to water" to wash off the sweat, dirt, and blood from the game.

One obligatory practice of Cherokee following a war expedition was to take part in the Victory Dance. In the old days upon their return, warriors carrying scalps would circle the townhouse, emitting war whoops to notify the community of their successful raid. Inside the house they would then smoke and recount their individual war deeds of heroism and valor.

The dance was continued by ballplayers, who would circle the dance area carrying feather wands in place of the scalps of earlier times. As the circling line of players gave out war whoops, the "dance driver" (leader) would suddenly point at some player with a stick and yell, "*ka!*" The circling would stop, while ballplayers gathered behind the designated man as he recounted his "game exploits." His athletic accomplishments would be recognized by war whoops of approval from fellow players, and the dance resumed until another was designated to relate his experiences on the field.

One of the many important components of the Cherokee warfare was their "sacred war fire." Returning warriors had to sit by the "war fire" for four days, passing their arms through the flames to cleanse them. On the warpath some

---

*John R. Swanton, "Social Organization and Social Usages of the Indians of the Creek Confederacy," in *Forty-second Annual Report of the Bureau of American Ethnology, 1924–1925* (Washington, DC: Government Printing Office, 1928), 461.

of the fire was actually carried with them in a pot (a "tote sack" or lantern could be used). Great care was taken that it never be extinguished, since it was needed on the return for purification rites. John Long, an Indian interpreter in the eighteenth century, reported that if the fire went out, the warriors would disperse and return to their homes. The fire is still an important part of lacrosse preparations, and players are cautioned to keep those from the opposing team from getting near it. If they get close enough, they might be tempted to "steal" from the fire, casually lighting a cigarette from it and bringing it back to their team conjurer, who might then use it to "fix" players on the other team.

The Warriors of the Ho-Chunk Nation Struggle on Home Turf (Ho-Chunk)

Occasionally the players in a legend are all depicted as humans. Representing the ancestors of the Ho-Chunk people in the following legend, the players are divided into two equal teams along traditional tribal lines. Many of the practices associated with warfare are part of the action—the proud boasting, for instance. The story also gives a picture of the old Indian version of the face-off.

The legend was collected by anthropologist Paul Radin, possibly from Sam or Jaspar Blowsnake, who wrote it down using the Winnebago syllabary from which Radin made his English translation sometime during the period 1908–13. He identifies the storyteller only as "a member of the bear clan."

Formerly known as the Winnebago, the Ho-Chunk or "The People of the First Voice," or "Big Fish" or "Primordial Fish" in their tongue, are linguistically a Siouan tribe, though since the eighteenth century they have shared much of their traditional material culture with Algonquian-speaking Woodlands neighbors, such as the Ojibwe. The ancestors of today's Ho-Chunk moved north, arriving in Wisconsin about 700 AD. Their first contact with Europeans was with the French in the early seventeenth century; by 1640, following three massive smallpox epidemics and warfare with neighboring tribes, only a few hundred survived. Originally they were organized into 12 patrilineal clans, divided into two moieties, Sky and Earth clans. In treaty land cessions in the nineteenth century, the Ho-Chunk lost all of their territory and in 1865 some were moved to northeastern Nebraska to a reservation. Others refused to move from Wisconsin, and some later moved back to former Ho-Chunk communities, seeking employment.

Paul Radin was one of the foremost authorities on the culture of the Ho-Chunk. A student of Franz Boas at Columbia, his principal fieldwork was at Winnebago, Nebraska, from 1908 to 1913. By consulting elders of the tribes, he attempted to reconstruct their precontact religion and mythology, as well as their ceremonial calendar. His principal informants were the Blowsnake brothers, Sam and Jaspar. Most of his information was first dictated and written down in the Winnebago syllabary, then translated by Oliver LaMere.

> The Wangeregi [Those Who Are Above] and the Manegi [Those Who Are on Earth] people agreed to play lacrosse. So the Wangeregi took an invitation stick and attached some tobacco to it and sent it to the Manegi people. Thus they fixed a day for the contest. The contest was to be in four days. In the meantime both sides were to get ready, for some players might be without balls or sticks. Then the Wangeregi said, "We are the faster runners and will therefore go and look for food." When they returned, the leader of the Wangeregi said again, "We are the fleeter and will therefore win from our opponents. In addition to that we are holy, and for that reason we will be strengthened in the coming contest." Then the leader of the Manegi said, "I will first pour tobacco and then I will arise with the blessing of life which was bestowed upon me and through which I know my men will be strengthened." Then they arranged the lacrosse goals, the *wakarani,* and arranged for the points. Then they took an emetic and went into a vapor bath in order to strengthen themselves. The goals were now standing far apart from each other.
>
> Then the people who were to play gathered on the field and warriors from each side began to tell their war exploits. First, one of the Wangeregi men told how he had cut off an enemy's head; how proud his sisters had been at receiving the gifts, and how they had danced in the Victory Dance. "With such a man you will have to play," he shouted to those on the other side. Then a man from the Manegi said, "I also am a brave man. I did with the enemy as I pleased. Once, when an enemy had been killed between the firing lines, I rushed for him, and in the midst of bullets I cut off his head. With such a man you will have to fight," he shouted to those on the other side. Then he gave a whoop, and the ball was thrown into the air and they began to play lacrosse. Those who

first succeeded in putting the ball through the *wakarani* four times would be declared the winners. All day they played, and in the evening then they stopped. Lacrosse was the favorite game among the Winnebago. This is all.

Source: *Paul Radin, "The Winnebago Tribe,"* 37th Annual Report of the Bureau of American Ethnology, 1915–1916 *(Washington, DC: Government Printing Office, 1923),* 72–73.

Despite the brevity of this legend, it contains a great deal of information. Many of the practices mentioned were fairly universal among tribes playing lacrosse. Consider how the story begins. The Ho-Chunk population was divided into two groups of people, and one side decides to challenge the other to a game. Typically, such a challenge would have been between villages of the same tribe, or in this case between the two tribal divisions. Or it might have been between different tribes to settle, say, some territorial dispute, like the Choctaw/Creek game in 1790 to determine tribal rights to a disputed beaver pond. The Creek won the game, but then the infuriated Choctaw players, joined by their warriors, attacked the Creek. It was reported that by the end of the following day, 500 were dead.

In the legend the challenge is set in motion by sending an "invitation stick" with tobacco tied to it. Such sticks were carried by runners from one community to another as a symbolic way of inviting or challenging them to some event—in this case a game, although invitation sticks in some situations were also used to assemble people for a religious ceremony.

Attaching tobacco to the invitation stick gave it a sort of "seal of approval," confirming that the challenge was in earnest. Tobacco in American Indian culture accompanies many such actions—gift-giving, for instance. It was also used to express appreciation. Whenever a canoe builder took bark off a birch tree, he always put a small amount of tobacco at the foot of the tree to give thanks to the spirit of the tree for allowing its bark to be taken. Similarly, tobacco always accompanied a request for someone to perform a task or teach some traditional knowledge or craft. In asking an elder to give an Indian name to your child, you always brought tobacco, or if you wanted someone to teach you his songs, you gave him tobacco. (The form of the tobacco offering was unimportant—it could be just a single cigarette, a plug of pipe tobacco, or even a tin of snuff.)

Once a lacrosse challenge was accepted—rarely was it turned down for the shame it would bring to a community—leaders of the two sides (or their delegates) then conferred to agree in advance on all aspects of how the game should be staged: when and where it would be held, how many players would be allowed per side, and how long the contest would go on. In the Ho-Chunk legend they "arranged for the points," that is, they decided how many goals one side needed to score to win. In this way, Indian lacrosse games were played in a kind of "sudden death" manner. In the Ho-Chunk game between the Wangeregi and Manegi they would play until one side had scored four goals.

The unit of four appears in many legends. That number has ritual significance among Native Americans, just as the number three has for Christians because of the Trinity. Certain ceremonial songs were performed sequentially in groups of four, and some of their melodies were required to be sung four times through. The number four also has symbolic connotations in nature; the four cardinal directions, or the four seasons. When the Ojibwe dance in a large circle around the central drum arbor over the singers in a powwow setting, their direction is clockwise. This is considered to be honoring the birth of the Four Winds as told in legend, beginning in the East, then South, West, and North.

In this tale it is not only the magic number of goals needed to win but also the number of days the players would wait before coming together for the contest. The pause was intended to allow teams time to get their game equipment ready, giving players a chance to replace missing balls and sticks. Of course, to make a new traditional stick today, the Ho-Chunk craftsman would need more than four days for the white ash wood to dry, once it was bent to shape and before netting was added. But in legends time is flexible, and things can be accomplished quickly. (See "A Dog's Power Beats the Old Chief" in chapter 1, where the traditional Iroquois hickory stick needed time to season.)

Most of this Ho-Chunk legend deals with preparations—nothing of the action in the game itself is even mentioned. The sides begin with considerable boasting. First, the Wangeregi claim their players to be faster than their opponents and send them off to get food, probably for a feast in conjunction with the game. Most members of each community would be expected to attend as spectators. Those who traveled some distance to the challenger's home would need to be fed. Acting as hosts for the event, the challengers would be expected to provide food and lodging for their visitors. If there was to be a rematch, as was often the case, the other community was expected to do likewise.

The Wangeregi continue to brag that their fast runners would be certain to win the game for them. Not only speed but bravery is brought up as a quality their players possess; here the close association between Indian lacrosse and warfare is evident. Cherokee ball-game scholars have suggested that a game challenge could have been a figurative declaration of war.

In the Creek language the word for lacrosse means literally "younger brother of war," and a former Creek player, James Hill, was explicit in his comparison of the game to fighting: "Match game pretty near like war, like United States make war 'gainst 'nother nation, like whip Philippines [in 1898]."* Equally explicit were the instructions of one Cherokee referee at the face-off before a game in the 1940s for the players not to play too roughly. "We goin' play ball—only a small war, not a big war." Like other scholars, James Mooney, who wrote about the Eastern Cherokee ball game and provided our first photographs of lacrosse, considered that the expression "play ball against them" was figuratively used for a contest of any sort, but particularly a battle.

Players in the legend are referred to as "warriors." Before the game men from each side recount their "war exploits," or the details of personal combat experiences. Each tries to outdo the other in boasting. (In William Stone's biography of the great Seneca leader Red Jacket, he tells how Iroquoian warriors were often chosen on the basis of their athletic skills shown by their performance on the lacrosse field.) First, the Wangeregi warrior relates how he cut off an enemy's head—formerly a war badge of honor, proof of being victorious on the warpath. The warrior tells how his sisters had been proud of him when he presented them with "gifts"—probably plunder taken from the enemy—and that they had celebrated his success in the Victory Dance.

The Victory Dance was always held back at one's home village to celebrate the victorious return of a community's warriors. Women in the Victory Dance, also called a "Scalp Dance" or "Squaw Dance," carried enemy scalps stretched on large hoops and mounted on poles. This performance was sometimes called "Dancing the Scalps." A photo of Menominee lacrosse players standing in a circle shows them raising their lacrosse sticks, whose cups contain bits of hair, as though they were scalp hoops.

By relating details of his hand-to-hand combat, the warrior is taunting the

---

*Mary R. Haas, "Creek Inter-town Relations," *American Anthropologist* 42 (1940): 483.

other side, predicting he will be just as brave in the forthcoming game. Not
to be outdone, a player from the opposing side brags that he is equally brave,
that he had the enemy "in the palm of his hand." As evidence he notes that he
had courageously "counted coup" on the enemy—that is, he had been able to
rush up to an enemy in the thick of battle and touch him without being injured or captured in doing so. In the story, a Wangeregi warrior describes
how, with bullets flying all around him, he cut off and retrieved the head of
an enemy body lying in no man's land.

Back-and-forth bragging and taunting between teams was typical behavior of Indian lacrosse players. The Dakota (Sioux), who formerly lived west of
the Ho-Chunks in territory that became the state of Wisconsin, spoke a language related to Ho-Chunk. Only the eastern bands of Sioux (Santee) played
lacrosse, and it is likely that they learned the game from the Ho-Chunk or
Ojibwe. The artist Francis B. Mayer attended and sketched Dakota games in
present-day Minnesota and noted the taunting that preceded them. Led by a
chief, each team marched to the lacrosse field "shouting loud whoops of
defiance to their opponents."

In the legend, when the "leader" of the Wangeregi (captain of the team)
returns with provisions, he reminds his opponents once again that his men
can run faster than those of the Manegi team and predicts that they will win
on that account. He raises the stakes in boasting that additionally his team is
"holy." By this he means that the various protective spirits, of which each man
had his own—usually some bird or animal—would look down upon the players with favor, promising them added powers to win. These protective spirits
first appeared to a young man during his "vision quest," when he was fasting,
isolated in the woods. Thereafter, he could always count on the spirit's protection, on the lacrosse field or on the warpath.

In the legend, the leader of the Wangeregi further intimidates their opponents by indicating he will "pour tobacco" on himself to insure their victory
as his team continues to seek additional blessings and powers. After this, men
from both sides set up the goal post at either end of the field agreed upon—
presumably the home field of the challengers. Then all the players submit to
certain physical preparations designed to cleanse and purify them. These are
believed to increase their strength, namely through an emetic (purgative)
and a "vapor bath" (sweat bath), designed to "cleanse" a player both internally
and externally. Often these preparations were identical to those used prior to
departure for battle as a means of protecting warriors. Similar ritual prepa-

rations were used before religious ceremonies as a means of purifying participants for the important spiritual event.

THE ROLE OF THE MEDICINE MAN IN LACROSSE

The players in this Ho-Chunk legend take sweat baths and emetics before
meeting to play. Although not specifically mentioned here, a medicine man,
or conjurer, would have supervised such cleansing rituals (see figure 1). In
most lacrosse communities these special practitioners were in charge of all
aspects of the game, particularly where supernatural means were required to
protect players and ensure their success in winning.

It is an ancient belief that supernatural forces were present in athletic
events. In the Greek Homeric verses, the god Apollo was described as directly
responsible for a contestant's winning or losing an athletic event. If an archer
missed his target, it was believed to be due to his failure to give a sacrifice
to Apollo. Similarly, if a charioteer dropped his whip, Apollo had probably
grabbed it from his hand.

In American Indian cultures the medicine man served much the same
function as Apollo. He appears in legends in his customary role as team doctor or coach in the preparation of every game. In one Ojibwe legend about the
origins of lacrosse, a boy falls asleep in his canoe and dreams of a large crowd
preparing a feast prior to a lacrosse game. On entering a wigwam (probably
a *mitewigan,* or medicine lodge), he finds a conjurer "preparing medicine for
a great game," by holding lacrosse sticks over smoke from a "medicine fire" to
ensure his team's success.

The Cherokee medicine man was particularly influential. His services were
considered essential, and he expected to be paid for them, so naturally the
players sought out the very best practitioners. As anthropologists James
Mooney and Frans M. Olbrechts aptly described it, "the whole affair takes the
aspect of a contest between the occult power of the two medicine men con-
juring for the teams . . . and the victory or defeat is laid at the door of the
medicine man rather than that the players themselves are congratulated or
scorned for it."* Once a Cherokee team had hired a medicine man, he was

---

*James Mooney and Frans M. Olbrechts, "The Swimmer Manuscript: Cherokee Sacred Formu-
las and Medicinal Prescriptions," *Bureau of American Ethnology Bulletin Number 99* (Washington, DC: Government Printing Office, 1932), 91–92.

paid in money or goods (shoes, clothing). The team was also expected to provide the materials he required in his rituals, such as divining (predicting) beads (see figure 1), or "old tobacco." The person sent to arrange the contract terms with the other team was not supposed to be a player, for fear that his temptation to brag would leave them vulnerable to spells from the opposing sorcerer. Once his service had been contracted, it was considered to be a "toehold."

The Cherokee ballgame conjurer inherited his position from the powerful medicine man who formerly accompanied war parties. Such an individual was responsible for measuring (divining) the enemy's strength and assisting with battle strategies. His services of course declined with the end of Cherokee warfare with Americans and other tribes at the end of the eighteenth century, but his role continued on into lacrosse well into the twentieth century.

These practices seem to have a long history. Although the Jesuits in Huronia were always suspicious of native conjurers, they never got close enough to see how they operated. Still, they were clearly aware of the medicine man's involvement in scheduling games to cure the sick. Tribes besides the Cherokee had similar figures. The Menominee member of the medicine lodge in charge of games always feared the powers of his opposing figure "to carry along the power of the sticks," that is, to cast spells on the lacrosse equipment. If that happened, he had means "to bring back the sticks," meaning to restore their power.

Conjurers had various means of bringing success to their team. The Yuchi medicine man could induce a pregnant woman to circle the goalposts to prevent scoring, and the Bad River Ojibwe living at Odanah had a medicine man to "doctor" balls. A Red Cliff player, Franklin Basina, described what happened at a 1950 game against Bad River. "Two old Odanah squaws were guarding the Red Cliff post; we couldn't score. That's when they were throwing in their *jiibik* [magic or doctored] balls. One on each side, post was in the middle, and they were standing at each side on the back of it. And there was a water puddle in back of them. It must have rained there a couple of days, and one of our boys said, 'I'll get rid of one of them old squaws. I'll see if I can knock the ball out of her, when she throws it.' Knock it out, you know, just knock it in that water. So when that ball gets in that water, that ball is no good. That kills their spirit. Them two squaws, they killed that ball. That ball was no good, she had to throw it out. [But] she didn't throw it out. I imagine she took it back home and gave it to the medicine man to work over it [to restore its former power]."*

In preparation for a game, the medicine man supervised the cleansing rituals for players, prepared emetics for them, and tied special bird feathers in their hair (see figure 1). He chose birds such as the hummingbird or the pee-wee because of their darting and running abilities. He assisted the players in attaching small wrapped pieces of bat wing at the base of their sticks' cups, acknowledging the legend of the birds and animals (chapter 1). Bat wings were attached as well to the rattle handles of the singer for the ballgame dance and onto the scaffold where the sticks rested the night before the game. The conjurer had special powerful formulas to recite, such as one called "This is to doctor the ball sticks to be able to pick up the ball." The words of that magic formula referred to the flying red bat, red being the color of war. He collected pieces of wood from a tree struck by lightning, reducing them to charcoal for players to paint on their bodies, giving them the power to "strike with the force of a thunderbolt."

Although the identity of a team's medicine man may have been kept secret, he remained present during the game, if not directly on the sideline, then probably somewhere nearby "making medicine." Because the medicine man was believed to be in control of the movement of lacrosse sticks and balls, one means for the Cherokee medicine man to increase his team's chances of scoring was to place behind the opponent's goal a dish containing the hide of a bull turtle, "to take the ball home." The ball was believed attracted to the dish like turtle to water. Or he could hold some of the sacred fire in his pipe, smoking behind the goal and blowing smoke to attract the ball. At Creek ceremonial games today, one can see the team's medicine man shaking his rattle behind the goal. A doctored ball with a hidden inchworm was likewise attracted to the medicine man behind the goal. Choctaw medicine men would hold mirrors from the sidelines to reflect the rays of the sun onto players during the game, which was believed to increase their strength. One Creek medicine man was noted for his ability to control the weather. One time, when his team was about to lose, he pulled "the last trick from his repertoire," causing a violent rainstorm. The game was called, and the rush to retrieve the wagers

*Franklin Basina, interview by Thomas Vennum, Lacrosse Transcripts, Archives of the Center for Folklife and Cultural Studies, Smithsonian Institution, Washington, DC.

sparked several hours of rioting. Although the medicine man's identity was supposedly kept secret, a clergyman in mid-nineteenth-century Georgia, Rev. George White, was pretty certain he could identify him in the crowd of spectators. The old man he suspected he guessed to be over a hundred years old; he sat near the center of the sidelines, and his hands appeared to be fumbling with shells and snake bones. As he relates the story in *Collections of Georgia* (1854), the elder refused to talk, and an angry looking Indian woman next to him dismissed the intruder saying, "Go away, white man!"

In the cleansing preparations to induce vomiting, a medicine man would boil certain plants in water to obtain their medicinal substances. One Iroquoian emetic used in present-day upstate New York was a potion made by boiling spotted alder with red willow. In Alabama, a Yuchi town chief prepared a protective formula by boiling buttonsnake root with red root that he kept in a special pot. The liquid was believed to be a gift from the Sun, and the pot was decorated with sun symbols. Players drank from the pot in a special ritual held at noon, when the sun was at its highest and could best bestow the benefits of its strongest rays on players. Four players at a time drank from the pot, while facing east, the direction from where the sun rises.

Such vomit-inducing liquids as well as other salves and ointments rubbed on players' bodies were intended to purify the men for a game. Reaching a "pure" state would help them avoid injuries and perform at full strength. A certain Creek medicine man, known for the potency of his potions made from "wolf tracks" and a "crayfish burrow," was once hired by a Choctaw team to perform the ritual by rubbing some of his magic liquid on the Choctaw players' bodies. This enabled them to win the game, keeping their opponents to a single goal.

The emetics were followed by a sweat bath, causing the players to perspire and thereby rid their bodies of impurities through the skin. (Sweat bath treatments were commonly turned to for other ailments as well—rheumatism, for instance, or lameness.) Like in today's steam bath or sauna, the naked players would sprinkle water on red-hot rocks to produce the vapor needed to effect a cure.

Cherokee warfare against other tribes and Europeans was pretty much at an end by 1800, and anthropologist Raymond Fogelson sees the ballplayers continuing the ritual behavior formerly practiced by warriors. For instance, during the Victory Dance, in place of the warpath stories, players would relate things they had accomplished during the lacrosse game, while teammates still shouted whoops of approval. The dance concluded with the distribution of cash, goods, and clothing to those who had sponsored it.

With the end of warfare, Fogelson sees the ball game as an outlet for the natural male tendency toward aggression. He guesses that lacrosse matches at that time were probably much more violent than games today. Fogelson also interprets the individualistic style of Cherokee one-on-one aggressive performance on the lacrosse field as a continuation of the former style of hand-to-hand combat on the warpath.

Even today, in Cherokee lacrosse all sorts of physical aggression are permissible—tackling, tripping, charging. Many of James Mooney's photographs show Cherokee players tied up in wrestling on the ground, going at it one-on-one (see plate 4). They may have thrown their sticks aside or turned them over to a referee to hold for them while they "duke it out." And southeastern tribes were not alone in permitting such violent behavior. In lacrosse of the Cayuga, one of the six nations of the Iroquois Confederacy, slashing was permitted so long as the player had both hands on his stick.

SYMPATHETIC MAGIC AND "SCRATCHING"

Emetics and sweat baths were but two of the preparations Indian lacrosse players faced. All of these procedures were carried out under the direction of the medicine man, in effect acting as a sort of coach. He administered potions and brews made from certain herbs and plants to spread on their bodies. In one particularly painful ordeal of certain southern tribes, the player submitted to "scratching" with an implement containing several rattlesnake fangs embedded into a handle like teeth of a comb, only spread more widely apart. Called *kanuga* in Cherokee, this "surgical tool" was applied by the medicine man on the limbs and chest of the player, with as many as a hundred or more strokes. (Since the procedure brought blood to the surface, it was also medically prescribed to cure high blood pressure and rheumatism.)

When performed on lacrosse players, "scratching" had a supernatural purpose—something anthropologists call "sympathetic magic." Tribal peoples in North America believe that by attaching a piece of an animal or bird to the player, somehow the attributes or characteristics of the creature are (magically) transferred to the player, enabling him to perform with talents the various creatures possessed. For example, Cherokee players would wear the feather of a wild turkey in their hair for games (see figure 1). The wild turkey

CHOCTAW NAMES TO DESCRIBE PLAYER SKILLS (OR LACK THEREOF)

canasa	moccasin snake
opa niskin	owl eyes
palki	fast player
sala'na wasona	slow player
siti	snake

Source: *Kendall Blanchard*, The Mississippi Choctaw at Play *(Urbana: University of Illinois Press, 1981), 37.*

is known for its running speed and also for its long-windedness. By having the feather in his hair, it was believed the player would gain these capacities. Similarly, Cherokee players would weave a bat's wing into the webbing of their lacrosse sticks. Because of the bat's great ability to dodge, dart, and escape being stopped, this would allow the player to perform in the same manner when on the lacrosse field. In another example of sympathetic magic, players would bathe with water in which a plant called "small rush" had been boiled. Because small rush always springs back into position when trampled underfoot, bathing in the solution would enable players to get right back up on their feet if knocked over.

The same belief system underlying sympathetic magic was behind certain prohibitions or taboos, called *gaktunka* in Cherokee. For instance, Eastern Cherokee players were expressly forbidden to eat rabbit. The rabbit, a timid animal, is easily spooked; contact with the rabbit might frighten a player, causing him to run in the crazy manner of rabbits. Also, players were not to handle babies, because they are weak and their bones are brittle. Ignoring this restriction, it was believed, potentially exposed one to broken limbs in a game.

One reason for scratching players was to create open wounds to absorb healing ointments and lotions that transferred the powers of the plants used in boiling down the lotions. The Cherokee medicine man used the plant "knife blade" to create his lotions because the leaves had a very sticky surface. Through sympathetic magic this would help a player hold onto his sticks in the rough and tumble of the game or to grab an opponent and hang onto him. Similarly a decoction of "great bulrush" was used because its hollow stem, it was believed, would improve a player's breathing.

By the end of the nineteenth century, southeastern tribes were making "scratchers" by substituting steel straight pins or turkey leg bone splinters for the rattlesnake fangs. But when snake fangs were used, it was thought the player could then strike his opponent with the speed and suddenness of a rattlesnake. Similarly, charcoal from a tree hit by lightning was used to draw sacred designs on a player, allowing him to strike opponents with the force of lightning.

The Yuchi scratching procedure was regarded as a form of protective inoculation and was derived from a Yuchi legend in which Sun is taken to Rainbow to be scratched. The blood that fell on the earth from that scratching was said to have turned into the first Yuchi.

THE INDIAN FACE-OFF

To begin the game in the Ho-Chunk legend "the ball was thrown in the air." The game begins after the Manegi man has bragged about counting coup, then he gives out a whoop and tosses up the ball. This way of setting the ball in motion at midfield to start a game and again after each goal seems unusual to nonnative players accustomed to today's face-off, where the ball stays on the ground. It is fought over by face-off specialists from each team; with their sticks held on the ground on either side of the ball, they wait for the referee's whistle to gain control of the ball.

Almost all reports on Indian games of the past described the toss-up as common practice, and it is still found today (see plate 3). Oklahoma Creek players from each side form a line across the end of the field and march shoulder to shoulder as a line to meet their opponents at centerfield, standing to face them about five yards apart. Then, a medicine man holding the small hide-covered ball in his hand paces back and forth between the two lines of players, singing a ritual chant. Without warning, he stops chanting and tosses the ball high above him. As it descends to the ground, it is fought over, particularly by those designated as "center-players." If skillful, one of them catches it mid-air, then runs with it or passes to a teammate. Usually, however, the small ball falls to the ground, where it is scrambled for until someone has retrieved it with his two sticks.

A similar practice is described in the Ho-Chunk game in this legend. Some tribes had a singer who accompanied himself on a small drum at midfield, next to a referee, who would toss up the ball. Franklin Basina, a northern Wisconsin Ojibwe, remembered that, as soon as the ball was tossed up, the singer would stop abruptly, "and he'd get the hell out of there!"

Instead of a toss-up, something approaching today's face-off may have been practiced by Iroquois. Since the Mohawk game is the ancestor of many of today's field games, possibly this was copied or adapted from them. An eye-witness to a Mohawk-Seneca game in 1897 in New York, Samuel Woodruff tells how players from each side advanced to midfield, while ten men were assigned to guard each goal. Apparently the ball was on the ground and was raised pinched between the sticks of a player from each side "to such an elevation as gave a chance for a fair stroke" (hit with the webbing of the stick?). Woodruff concludes by saying "much depends on the first stroke, and great skill is exerted to obtain it." (His description seems closer to "the draw" in today's women's game than to the face-off.) The historian Lewis Henry Morgan in his *League of the Iroquois* (1851) described a slightly different Mohawk practice that seems to resemble what a hockey referee does in throwing down the puck on the ice. In a game beginning about noon, the "center players" formed two parallel lines, then the ball was dropped between the lines. Hewitt's report on Iroquoian lacrosse in 1892 suggests something resembling today's face-off. As the two team captains held their sticks in the form of a Maltese Cross, the ball was placed "mid way between the ends of the network on each club; then by a steady push each captain endeavors to throw the ball in the direction of the goal to which his side must bear it."*

*Lewis Henry Morgan, *League of the Ho-de-no-sau-nee or Iroquois* (Rochester, 1851; reprint, ed. Herbert M. Lord, New York: Dodd, Mead & Co., 1904), 295; J. N. B. Hewitt, "Iroquois Game of Lacrosse," *American Anthropologist* 5 (1892): 191.

PLATE 1.
A young right-handed Seneca player in 1901 using typical Iroquoian stick of the period, apparently "playing catch" with another person off camera. Note the wide-spaced webbing of the stick. He wears the Iroquoian *ga-ka* loincloth, moccasins, and headband with a rear feather.

Photograph by Alanson B. Skinner, courtesy of the National Museum of the American Indian, Smithsonian Institution

PLATE 2.

An Eastern Cherokee line of players in 1908 preparing to march to centerfield carrying items they will wager, such as handkerchiefs and blankets. Note the muslin shorts, bare feet, and kerchiefs tied around players' necks. The star on shorts of the player second from the left designates a "star" player. Nonplaying supporters behind the line will follow them in "taking out the bets."

Photograph by Col. Frank C. Churchill, courtesy of the National Museum of the American Indian, Smithsonian Institution

PLATE 3.
A typical face-off of Eastern Cherokee "center fighters" in 1908 waiting for the ball to descend from being tossed in the air, probably by the man in long pants in the foreground. Note the player on the left holding his two sticks together like a baseball batter, preparing to swat the ball downfield to a teammate, hence the name "center knocker."

Photograph by Col. Frank C. Churchill, courtesy the National Museum of the American Indian, Smithsonian Institution

PLATE 4.

Two pairs of opponents in 1907 wrestling on the playing field—a common practice in Eastern Cherokee lacrosse, not an infraction. The action appears to be downfield, as players and fans alike seem to be rushing in that direction. Note the feathers tied in the hair of two players (cf. figure 1).

Photograph by Col. Frank C. Churchill, courtesy of the National Museum of the American Indian, Smithsonian Institution

PLATE 5.
Mississippi Choctaw player Albert Henry with his pair of sticks in 1918. Homemade, their lengths are determined by the distance between the player's fingers and the ground. One stick is made shorter, its cup smaller, to contain the ball when running with it (see figure 6). The player wears pieces of the Choctaw "national costume," such as the skullcap with a feather at its top. Not visible is unquestionably a "tiger tail" of some sort that would extend up the player's behind (see plate 8). Note the bare feet and the pants cuffs secured for ease in play. Only the front of this ornament is visible—the cloth crotch cover, held in place by a belt.

Photograph by Mark R. Harrington, courtesy of the National Museum of the American Indian, Smithsonian Institution

PLATE 6.

A Florida Seminole player tossing a ball with his pair of sticks in 1910. He wears typical dress of his tribe. As with all southeastern players he uses two sticks in tandem. These wooden sticks are unusual, being carved with closed cups instead of the more typical open frame with rawhide thongs (see figure 7), and apparently uniquely Seminole. Because some early European reports on the game described the sticks as "ladles," perhaps they had Seminole lacrosse in mind.

Photograph by Alanson B. Skinner, courtesy of the National Museum of the American Indian, Smithsonian Institution

PLATE 7.

Four Menominee men and a boy posed for a photograph in 1917. The mixed-race crowd behind them and their wearing priceless elaborate beadwork on bandolier bags, turbans with eagle feathers, and beaded knee bands suggests they may be participants in some exhibition powwow. Such elaborate attire was atypical of what Menominee wore when playing lacrosse. They were probably dance props, like the war club held by the man on the far left. Such trophy items would be carried as part of a dancer's regalia as he circled the powwow drum arbor.

Photograph by Alanson B. Skinner, courtesy the National Museum of the American Indian, Smithsonian Institution

PLATE 8.

"Fat Tom," A Mississippi Choctaw in 1908 holding his pair of sticks and wearing the traditional skullcap, minus its customary feather. His "tiger tail" ornament strapped to his buttocks is a twentieth-century version of the horsehair tails George Catlin painted on the Choctaw players at Fort Gibson in 1832 (see figure 16).

Photograph by Mark R. Harrington, courtesy the National Museum of the American Indian, Smithsonian Institution

4

Tricksters and Culture Heroes

Traditional cultures throughout the world tell stories populated with legendary creatures, both good and bad. Many of these societies have assigned a hero's role to a central figure, who although mythical is regarded somehow as the ancestor of those listening to the tales of his adventures (or misadventures). These benevolent characters are called "culture heroes," having brought all good things to humans, including their religion, and having taught them how to hunt and plant and therefore survive.

Sometimes the culture hero is cast in the role of a trickster who, although he creates things, also destroys. Totally at the mercy of his passions, the trickster's lewd behavior often lands him in trouble, much to the delight of the narrator's audience.

American Indian oral narrative is represented by many legends about tricksters and culture heroes. It is not surprising to find episodes where they play games of some sort together with humans (and other mythical creatures). In some tribes, of course, that includes lacrosse.

The next three legends belong to three tribes whose traditional homeland is in the western Great Lakes—the Ho-Chunk (Winnebago), Menominee, and Ojibwe. The Ho-Chunk live in present-day southwestern Wisconsin and northeastern Nebraska and are linguistically a Siouan tribe (for more on them, see "The Warriors of the Ho-Chunk Nation Struggle on Home Turf" in chapter 3). The Menominee, whose traditional home lands were near Green Bay in northeastern Wisconsin, are Algonquian speakers (see chapter 2, "The First Lacrosse Ball"). So too are their neighbors to the west, the Ojibwe of Wisconsin, whose communities extend into Minnesota and southwestern Ontario (see chapter 3, "Wakayabide Is Killed Playing Lacrosse").

He Who Wears Human Heads for Earrings Defeats the Giants (Ho-Chunk)

Many of the heroes in the legends of these three peoples are widely known throughout North America. They have their counterparts, known by different names. Elsewhere in America the trickster may be called Coyote, Spider, or Old Man. The plots of their tales are similar, and much of the detail in their escapades is identical from tribe to tribe. The Ho-Chunk have several culture heroes, among whom Red Horn, a noted warrior, is the most prominent.

The stories describing the heroes' adventures are all parts of the overall legend of the culture-hero figure. Narrators grouped their adventures into long units, or cycles. Within each tribe were a small number of talented storytellers with extraordinary memories. Only they possessed the right to tell these legends; the stories were considered part of their property (they "owned" them), so one paid accordingly to have the stories told—in cash, goods, or services. A particularly long cycle, to be told in its entirety, might need to be recited over time and paid for in installments.

To appreciate this tale, the reader needs to know where the episode fits into the longer cycle. The episode describing culture hero Red Horn's lacrosse game against evil giants is unusual in many respects. It is the only legend in this collection to feature women lacrosse players. It is also unique in the detailed account of the action of the game itself, which occupies a good part of the story.

The legend is the fifth episode in a lengthy cycle describing Red Horn's adventures. The youngest of ten sons, Red Horn begins by beating his brothers in a race, then sets out with them to search out and attack enemies. He is the first in his war party to obtain a "war honour"—that is, successfully kill or scalp an enemy—or even to "count coup," in which he dares to run up to an enemy and touch him, then escape without harm. Following his military victories, Red Horn is courted by Orphan Girl at her grandmother's urging, and in the episode following that he is able to pull an arrow from a wounded man and save his life.

At this point in the cycle, the lacrosse game takes place, when Red Horn and his teammates defeat and kill giants who have been plaguing residents of a neighboring village. Following the lacrosse victory, the giants somehow come back to life to challenge the hero's team to a series of further contests. The hero's team in turn is successful at playing dice, then at demonstrating shooting abilities and winning at "who can stay underwater the longest." Finally, Red Horn's team is defeated and killed at wrestling. In American Indian legends culture heroes never die, so the cycle continues with the hero's son taking revenge on his father's death and restoring him to life.

This tale, like "The Warriors of the Ho-Chunk Nation Struggle on Home Turf" (chapter 3), was collected by Paul Radin as part of his fieldwork in Winnebago, Nebraska, 1908–13. It was probably written down by either Sam or Jaspar Blowsnake.

Now, once again, the people cried, "Here are some men coming this way who are weeping." So all went to the edge of the village to see them. The latter got nearer and nearer, carrying a sacred pipe ahead of them. When the men got very near they asked, "Where does the chief live?" "In the middle of the village, in that long lodge there, that is where he lives," said the people. "This is one of the chief's friends," they said, pointing to Turtle. Then the suppliants went toward Turtle and directed the stem of the pipe towards his mouth. "Ho!" said he. They told him that giants had come upon them and that they were coming to him for assistance to help them against these giants. Then Turtle went home and constructed a drum and all night they heard him drumming. His friends, however, said, "We need not go there until he calls." So they stayed away. But he did not call them. In the morning, he went out but his friends did not go along, so that very few indeed followed him. What could he do with these few followers? The result was that those who had asked for help were beaten again.

Some evenings afterwards it was said, "They are coming again." One of the villagers, however, asked the newcomers why they didn't call upon the chief who lived at the end of the village beyond. So they went there and found Turtle in the chief's house. They suspected, however, that

Turtle was there on purpose, so they directed the pipe towards Red Horn. But the latter said, "My friend, you smoked it for them before, you may smoke it again." "Ho!" said Turtle, and the pipe was stuck into his mouth. Turtle made a drum again and danced that night. In the morning they went to encounter the giants. The one who was helping the giants most was a giantess with red hair, just like Red Horn's hair. Turtle said to Red Horn, "My friend, the giantess has hair just like yours and she is the one that is securing victory for her people because she is a very fast runner. When they play ball she does all the work. Coyote and the Martin are also married to giantesses as those and these also greatly aid them."

On this occasion the chiefs had come along, so most of the people accompanied them and, consequently, they had many good runners.

Then said Turtle to Wolf, "My friend, let us go and match the ball-sticks." This they did accordingly, placing Red Horn's ball-stick together with that of the giantess so he might play against her. Storms as He Walks's stick was matched against that of a giant, Wolf's stick against that of Coyote, and Otter's against that of Martin. Just then, the giant chieftainess said, "When shall we ready to play ball? I am getting rather anxious." To which Turtle replied, "Just as soon as my friend comes we shall start." Then the chieftainess said, "Who is your friend that it takes him so long to come?" "Wait till he comes! You certainly will laugh when you see him." "Why, what is there funny about him that I should laugh?" said the giantess. "Just wait till he comes," said Turtle, "just wait till he comes, and then you will see."

Soon after that he came, and Turtle said to him, "My friend, let us go over there and look at the sticks of the ball players." "Very well," said he. They went and found the giantess there and, when she saw him, she most certainly laughed and bowed her head. "There you are," said Turtle. "I thought you said you would not laugh?" "Yes," said the giantess, "but I did not laugh at him." "Well," said Turtle, "look at him again." The giantess looked again and the small heads he was wearing in his ears stuck their tongues out at her. Again she laughed and bowed her head. Then Turtle made fun of her.

Soon after the people said, "Now, come, start the game." Then said Turtle to He Who Wears Human Heads as Earrings, "My friend, let us, you and I, start the game." So they gave a war-whoop and tossed the ball to the giants, while the others stood guard. Coyote was placed opposite Wolf. Then Turtle said to Red Horn, "As soon as the ball comes near, hit the giants' sticks." "Ho!" said Red Horn.

The ball was tossed up and when it came near the ground, Red Horn stuck his stick out, keeping the others away from Turtle. Turtle caught the ball. Then he ran among the giants swinging his stick. "Big black cowards," he said, "stand back or I will knock some of you down!" The giants' sticks rattled about him, but he came out with the ball. He threw the ball low, making it rise higher and higher. It lit just beyond where Wolf and Coyote were standing. Coyote seized it and started to run around the others. Turtle stood in the distance saying, "My friend is going to do something, my friend is going to do something!" He meant Wolf. Wolf watched Coyote very carefully and then struck him in the flank with his shoulders. Up in the air he sent him flying. Turtle gave a whoop as he saw this, for it was just what he wanted Wolf to do when he said, "My friend is going to do something." Turtle then got the ball again and sent it through the goal into the very midst of the giants. Thus they won the first point. Turtle shouted, "Come on! Come on! It is such fun to play ball!"

Again they played. This time Otter and Martin were the guardians of the goal. The ball was tossed up, and again Turtle got the ball and "whirled" into the midst of the giants. Getting clear, he threw the ball but it rose gradually as it went farther and lit just beyond the place where Otter and Martin were standing. Martin seized it and ran, but again Turtle shouted, "My friend is going to do something." Otter headed Martin off and, watching carefully, hit him in the flank with his shoulder, sending him into the air. "Oh dear, our son-in-law!" said the giants. Then Otter put the ball through the goal.

After this, Martin began to move about and got up, using his ball-stick as a cane. "Come! come! It is such fun to play ball!" they said, and the game was started again. Storms as He Walks and the giant chieftainess were together at the goal as before. Turtle caught the ball and whirled it into the midst of the giants. "You women, you big black cowards, stand back or I will knock some of you down," he said, and he whirled about. When he got clear he threw the ball low and let it rise, as it went farther and farther. Just where the giantess and Storms as He Walks stood, there it lit. Storms as He Walks got the ball and ran with it, the chieftainess after him. When she caught up with him, he ran harder and caused it to thunder. The chieftainess got frightened and jumped aside. Then Turtle gave a whoop in the distance and began poking all sorts of fun at the giantess. The mother of the latter said, "You good-for-nothing woman, hit him!" Again the giantess came near to him but, as he ran all the harder and thundered, she screamed and jumped back. Turtle, all this time, was having his usual fun on the side, shouting at her and poking fun at her. Finally, Storms as He Walks ran through the goal, winning another point. "Come on! Come on! It is such fun to play ball! Let us start again."

They gave a whoop and started again. Kunu [brother of Red Horn] and Turtle were at the throwing-off place. Turtle said, "My friend usually swings his stick pretty wide." And sure enough Kunu swung his stick in such a way as to interfere with the giant's stick, giving Turtle a chance to catch the ball which he did. And then, on getting clear of the giants Turtle threw the ball to the place where Red Horn and the giantess were standing. Red Horn got the ball and ran with it, the giantess after him. Turtle, as usual, began poking fun at her and shouting. Just as she caught up to Red Horn the latter turned about, and the little faces in his ears stuck out their tongues at her and the eyes winked at her. She was running with upraised stick but, when she saw the faces, she laughed and let down her stick. This made Turtle shout all the more. "My friend, look back at her; my friend, look back at her!" Then he gave whoops. The mother of the giantess was talking very excitedly, "That good-for-nothing woman, she is smitten with him! She will make the whole village suffer on her account!" And so Red Horn ran through the goal, winning the point. The giants were thus beaten in all four points. The giant chieftainess was whipped by her people because she lost the game on account of her falling in love with Red Horn.

The giants wanted to try again, and the chieftainess said, "I will match myself against Red Horn no matter what happens to me." Then the other chiefs, his friends, also matched themselves with the giant chiefs. Almost the whole village of giants was included and the only giants not included in these were some of the very old people. The game, however, again resulted in victory for Red Horn and his friends, the giants losing all the four points.

Then said Turtle, "My friend, something just occurred to me." "What is it?" they said. Then he said, "This giantess has the same color hair as my friend Red Horn, and I think that we ought to spare her life and let my friend here marry her." "Ho!" they exclaimed, "If that is your desire, then let it be as you wish." Thereupon they gathered together all the giants and placed them in four circles. Then they told the giantess that they had decided to spare her life. She was very grateful. Turtle then said, "If we were to kill all these one at a time, we would never get through, there are so many of them. So I think that we had better leave this to our friend, Storms as He Walks." Thus spoke Turtle. So Storms as He Walks went towards them with his club and struck the first circle. Then it thundered, and the thunderbirds above said, "Storms as He Walks is shooting. What can he be shooting at? He said that he liked the human beings." Then again for the second time it thundered. "Ho-o-o! What can Storms as He Walks be shooting at?" they said again. Then a third and fourth time it thundered. The thunderbirds said, "Surely he has shot something."

As soon as the Giants had been killed, the people left the place where the game had been played. They were living in the first village that had been attacked by the giants. "We are not being treated very well here, so let us go with you and live in your village," they said. So they went home with the victors.

Source: *Paul Radin, "A Study in Aboriginal Literature," in Indiana University,* Memoirs of the Anthropological Journal of Linguistics, *14, no. 3 (July 1948): 38.*

This colorful legend is set in ancient times when giants roamed the world, killing and eating humans. They are ultimately beaten (as good always wins out over evil) through the efforts of benevolent spirits and extraordinary human beings. Reminiscent of the great game between the birds and land animals (chapter 1), this legend features animals in the game, but here they have joined forces with humans. The creatures such as Wolf, Turtle, and Martin, as we have already seen, are "kings," or leading spirits, of each species, who guard over their representatives on earth and must be treated with respect.

The anonymous creators of this legend assigned animals to both teams: Martin and Otter play for the giants, but Wolf and Turtle are on Red Horn's team. These assignments are made before the game by matching the players' sticks. One senses the immediacy of the play-by-play action in this remarkable story—at times, the narrator is nearly as detailed in his observations as a current-day sportscaster.

TEAM SELECTION

In the legend, Turtle, who functions as a team captain or coach, suggests to Wolf, "Let us go and match the ball-sticks"—an old Indian practice to even up opponents and equalize team strength. Once the players for the giants have been matched up against Red Horn's team, the game is begun with a toss-up of the ball at centerfield, which in this story is called "the tossing-off place." A practice still found in the southeastern game, the toss-up functions exactly like today's face-off; it is performed again after each goal is scored. In the Red Horn game, the toss-up is preceded by a "war-whoop" to signal both teams that the ball is about to be put into play.

Although Red Horn is the hero, having scored the game-winning goal, other characters play significant roles—especially Turtle. He is the first one to be approached by the villagers for help against the giants. As "one of the chief's friends," he must be important; later, he is found by the visitors in the chief's lodge, the longest wigwam, of course.

Turtle is responsible for many of a coach's duties. He seems to be the team's organizer; the others will not follow until he calls. It is Turtle who has "scouted out" the opposition and is able to report back to Red Horn on their strengths—that the red-haired giantess is a fast runner and "does all the work" and that Coyote and Martin's wives are equally good players. In his preliminary conversation with the impatient giantess, Turtle stalls her by saying, "Just wait till he comes"—much as a college coach might boast to his counterpoint on the rival team, "Just wait until you see my new freshman attackman!"

Red Horn clearly looks up to Turtle; when the visitors present their pipe, Red Horn defers to Turtle to smoke. Turtle also functions as the players' spiritual leader, or medicine man—the one who makes the drum and dances all night before the game in ceremonies designed to bring his players success and prevent them from injuries. As such, he is in the same role as a priest in an ancient Greek temple, acting as go-between for the players and the god Apollo, who controls all athletic events.

Turtle is also the taunter; throughout the game he "pokes fun" at the giantess, having "his usual fun at the side[lines]." Even on the field he threatens opponents confidently: "Stand back, you black [evil] cowards, or I'll knock you down." He successfully distracts the giantess when Red Horn is about score, causing her to laugh and drop her stick.

The game is characterized by typically rough lacrosse play throughout. Martin is given a severe body-check by Otter—striking his flank by the shoulders with such force that he is "sent flying." The second time this happens, he is forced to limp off the field using his stick for a cane, causing his teammates, the giants on the sideline, to lament his injury, "Oh dear, our son-in-law!" The spectators are not immune from encouraging violence. The giantess's mother, disgusted by her daughter's performance in the game, yells, "You good-for-nothing woman, hit him!" like some impatient parent from the sidelines.

Whoever created the story had obviously seen or performed in many Ho-Chunk lacrosse games, for details of the action are very specific. Take, for instance, the point in the story after Turtle has scored the first goal. At the next toss-up, Turtle recovers the ball; even though he is crowded by giants, he breaks free, enough to rid himself of the ball with a long pass downfield. Unfortunately, it lands near Martin, playing for the giants. Martin intercepts, scoops the ground ball, and starts to run with it, but his defender, Otter, is dogging him and successfully "heads him off," giving him a violent body-check with the shoulder and sending him flying. Otter retrieves the ball and scores. Throughout this mayhem, the Red Horn's players are certainly having fun winning. Repeatedly they yell, "Come on! Come on! It is such fun to play ball!"—another taunt to their opponents.

WOMEN IN INDIAN LACROSSE

Red Horn's opponent in the game, the giantess with red hair, may be the only instance we can find of women playing lacrosse in traditional American Indian legends. Compared to the men's role in the game, there is very little documentation of Indian women's lacrosse. Creek women's games were photographed in the 1920s—a rare instance.

How should we interpret the fact that the giants' team has women as star players? Is it possible that long ago women were a valuable asset to a Ho-Chunk man's team, especially tall runners as in this story? The minimal information on women in the game may simply mean that playing lacrosse came to be regarded as an exclusively male activity, along with their other traditional roles in hunting and waging war.

Occasionally women are mentioned in the lacrosse accounts of travelers and researchers. One of our earliest sources, Lieutenant Henry Timberlake in 1765, confirms that Cherokee women played, as did Mooney's principal

Cherokee consultant in the game a century later, Will West Long. Long's mother had played a form of lacrosse, but using hands, not sticks. Walter J. Hoffman found a "mixed game" of the Dakota to be "very amusing," and in a 1968 interview Paul Buffalo, a Minnesota Leech Lake Ojibwe, remembered men and women playing and characterized it as "a rough game."

It seems when men played opposite women, adjustments in team numbers and field size were made. In the Dakota woman's game, which usually followed the men's event, sometimes men and women were on the same team, but when separated by gender, the Dakota permitted a five-to-one ratio of women to men. In Indian Territory, men with sticks opposed women using their hands, and the goals were moved closer together.

In place of lacrosse, Indian women of many tribes had their own games— forms of field hockey and shinny, for the most part. Ojibwe women played a double-ball game with pointed sticks on which they carried two balls connected by a rawhide thong. When they were little girls, women could pick up lacrosse from playing with their male friends. French fur trader Nicholas Perrot relates that in the eighteenth century Huron boys and girls learned lacrosse in childhood games, although his report is confusing about how the teams were made up; he writes only that "men and women, young boys and girls, all play on one side or the other." Thomas McKenney, first superintendent of Indian Affairs was at the east end of Lake Superior in July 1826; referring to Ojibwe children, he wrote, "the little naked Indians boys, and hardly better-clad girls, were meanwhile sporting over the green, playing ball— *bag-gat-iway* [the Ojibwe word for lacrosse]."* George Catlin's paintings of women's games of the Choctaw and Dakota show them to be every bit as exciting, congested, and rough as the men's games he depicted. His oil canvas of a Dakota woman's game confirms it was wagered on; a betting pole with colorful goods hanging from it is shown in the background, in front of which stream a mass of female players.

TURTLE AS COACH AND PLAYER

Elsewhere in the Red Horn cycle, Turtle is portrayed as something of a clown, or buffoon, but in this legend he takes a vital, serious role. He is shown as a

*Thomas L. McKenney, *Sketches of a Tour to the Lakes* (Baltimore: Fielding Lucas Jr., 1827), 180–81.

talented, dedicated leader of his players—a crucial factor in their winning. When the villagers requesting assistance first arrive at Red Horn's town, they naturally wish to see the chief, but it takes them another visit to understand it is Turtle who can help in lacrosse matters. They realize this after finding Turtle in the chief's lodge; when they offer the pipe to Red Horn, he defers to Turtle to smoke from it, in effect saying, "This is the guy you *really* need to deal with!"

Turtle is represented as the team's medicine man. He makes a drum and dances prior to their departure for the game, doubtless to petition the spirits. This shows him in charge of the team's spiritual protection, knowing the obligatory ritual preparations. His role as a coach is also apparent. He has scouted the opposition's strength, just as the Cherokee medicine man did accompanying a war party. Turtle also informs his players which ones on the other side to watch out for. He negotiates the beginning of the game and leads Red Horn "to look at the sticks" of their opponents, much in the way a lacrosse coach might take his star players to watch a scrimmage of some team they were about to play.

Turtle is at midfield to start the game with the toss-up, just as the Creek medicine man does today. Once the game is under way, Turtle's coaching role is clear. He instructs Red Horn to "hit the giants' sticks" as soon as he sees a ground ball. He directs Wolf to slam Coyote when he has a chance. This instruction causes Wolf to give Coyote the body-check that "sends him flying." As a coach, Turtle lets out a war whoop of congratulation, "for it was just what he had wanted Wolf to do."

When not actually playing, which he does well (he is the first to score for Red Horn's team)—on the sidelines Turtle behaves like any overly enthusiastic coach: he gives war whoops and taunts the other players, especially Red Horn's opponent, the giant redhead. After the giants lose in a rematch, it is Turtle who decides the losers' fate, that Storms as He Walks should do the "mop-up," that is, kill all the enemy with his war club.

STICK TECHNIQUES IN LEGENDS

We know virtually nothing about technique from the period in which these legends were invented. Despite so much other information imparted by the Red Horn story, there are few clues about ball-handling. Brief descriptions in the action of the game do help: "[Turtle] getting clear, he threw the ball but

FIGURE 11.
In "Sioux's Playing Ball" (1843) by American painter Charles Deas, the player on the right attempts to retrieve a ground ball using "the Indian scoop" but has his efforts blocked by the player on the left. Some players are barefoot; others have on moccasins. Note the feather bustle, face and body paint, and horsehair drops around the player's waist.

Photo courtesy the Gilcrease Museum, Tulsa, Oklahoma

it rose gradually as it went farther and lit [on the ground], and later "he threw the ball low and let it rise as it went farther and farther," where this time it "lit" next to Storms as He Walks, defended by the giantess. These descriptions suggest that the stick being described must have had some sort of pocket, enabling one to catch (up close, at least, in the toss-up) and throw.

The traditional Ho-Chunk wooden stick conforms to the style of most Great Lakes sticks (see figure 7). If Red Horn and his team were using fore-runners of this traditional stick, it did indeed have a pocket—but usually only several rawhide thongs crossed and tied at midpoint. This style of webbing was really only designed to keep the wooden ball from falling through the circular frame at the end of the handle, its diameter scarcely larger than that of the ball. It did, however, permit "scooping" up a ground ball with a quick flick of the wrist (figure 11).

That stick is crucially different from the Iroquoian stick and its plastic descendants, with their pocket at the throat of the large netted area, the webbing extending upward and outward in a "V" shape from the pocket. This aspect of its construction served to catch a passed ball from the air and, through the player's arm and hand control, instantly guide it into the snug security of the pocket.

That catching capacity is scarcely possible with the Great Lakes stick. It lacks anything approaching the surface area of the Iroquoian stick, which also precludes any passing with accuracy. As with the southeastern stick, the ball is thrown *in the general direction* where the player intends it to go—usually just downfield somewhere near the goal or a teammate. This can scarcely be described as accurate passing; it has predictably poor results: In throwing the ball, Turtle gives a long toss to Otter, the intended recipient, but his defender Martin gets the ball instead.

A few skilled Great Lakes Indians, but not many, were capable of catching a ball midair at a distance, as well as accurately hitting a distant target. The descriptions of stick handling in the legend suggest that what we are familiar with as the traditional Great Lakes stick was already being used when the legend was being formulated. The narrator's words imply their style of passing as actually *throwing*. Turtle "threw the ball *to the place* where Red Horn and the giantess were standing" (emphasis added). Instead, the Red Horn game stressed running as a desirable skill; it says nothing about passing. A player running with the Great Lakes stick held it out from his body horizontally with the ball cradled, waving it slightly from side to side.

A number of traditional Indian lacrosse practices noted in the other legends are touched on in Red Horn's story, among them the all-night ball game dance, "matching" the sticks before the game, war whoops at the toss-up and interspersed throughout. The warfare imagery of thunder and lightning is brought in. When the giantess is dogging Storms as He Walks, he causes it to thunder; frightened, she steps aside.

Despite the game's setting in the distant, mythological past, today's players will recognize some of the typical lacrosse action as well as the language to describe it in this legend. Kunu (Red Horn's brother) during the toss-up delivers a stick-check on a giant player so Turtle can catch the ball on its descent; Otter then slams him with a body-check.

Manabus Is Dogged by Waves (Menominee)

Moving from the Ho-Chunk in southwestern Wisconsin to the northeast of the state, we meet the Menominee culture hero, Manabus. Like all tricksters, he appears in stories that have unbelievable situations, many of them describing abnormalities or modes of behavior, which would spark the curiosity of Indian children in the storyteller's audience.

Indian elders used many trickster stories to explain to their children certain peculiarities of nature. Called "etiological" tales, they exist in all traditional cultures, where they fall into the category of "instructional stories"— an important part of a child's education. Examples abound in world culture— the "just so stories," such as "How the Leopard got his Spots" in sub-Saharan Africa and India. A Ho-Chunk legend explains why the beaver's paws are drawn together: The hero Hare (another trickster figure), while eating a beaver, forgets he is supposed to leave the sinews attached to the bones and in his haste to eat breaks some of them in the beaver's forepaw. In another legend, Hare knocks out Frog's formerly long front teeth for talking too much, thus explaining why frogs have no teeth.

In traditional Menominee beliefs, the mythical Manabus was a culture hero whose escapades enrich a large body of stories. Elders told these tales to their grandchildren, formerly around a central fire in the birch-bark wigwam, more recently before a wood-burning cast-iron stove in the family kitchen. Most stories were recounted during the winter months, when Indians in the harsh climate of snow, ice, and cold in the northern forests surrounding the western Great Lakes spent most of their time in wigwams and tepees. Because of their isolation and confinement indoors, children were a ready audience; storytelling kept them entertained. The stories were told in the wintertime also because the snakes and toads were dormant; asleep, it was believed, they could not overhear the people talking about them, become offended, and somehow "get even" by causing some misfortune to the storyteller once the weather improved. In Indian belief, to get even, a toad would jump on you in your sleep and cause welts on your body.

In the Manabus cycle of tales, Menominee elders recounted how their hero brought all good things to the Indians—taught them how to build their wigwams, hunt, and set their traps. His counterpart among the Ojibwe, the neighbors of the Menominee, was Wenaboozho, who with his grandmother was said to have discovered wild rice for their people. The Menominee, whose name derives from the Ojibwe word for wild rice (*manoomin*), were once active rice-harvesters, but when their reservation was created, tragically its boundaries excluded them from former ricing lakes. Traditionally, wild rice was an important food for both tribes—a vital source of energy to get them through the long winter—as well as a valuable commodity in the fur trade.

Manabus is also believed to have brought the Menominee their traditional religion as well as powerful medicine. Because this mythical character has many human qualities, he has his "naughty" side and is constantly getting into trouble. There are stories in which he generally causes riots. Although Manabus behaves and looks like a human in the stories, he is actually a spirit with great medicine powers. Thus he is able to change his outward appearance and even his being.

Now it happened that the beings above challenged the beings below to a mighty game of lacrosse. The beings below were not slow to accept the game, and the goals were chosen, one at Detroit and the other at Chicago. The center of the field was at a spot called Kesosasit ("where the sun is marked") [on the rocks] near Sturgeon Bay in Lake Michigan. The above beings called their servants—the thunderers, the eagles, the geese, the ducks, the pigeons, and all the fowls of the air—to play for them, and the great white underground bear called upon the fishes, the snakes, the otters, the deer, and all the beasts of the field to take the part of the powers below.

When everything was arranged and the two sides were preparing, Manabus happened along that way. As he strolled by, he heard someone passing at a distance and whooping at the top of his voice. Curious to see who it was, Manabus hastened over to the spot from where the noise came. Here he found a funny little fellow, like a tiny Indian, no other, however, than Nakuti, the sunfish. "What on earth is the matter with you?" asked Manabus. "Why, haven't you heard?" asked Sunfish, astonished. "Tomorrow there is going to be a ball game, and fishes and the beasts of the field will take the part of the powers below against the

Thunderers and all the fowls, who are championing the powers above."
"Oh ho!" said Manabus, and the simple Nakuti departed, whooping with
delight. "Well, well," thought Manabus, "I must see this famous game,
even if I was not invited."

The chiefs of the underworld left their homes in the waters and
climbed high up on a great mountain where they could look over the
whole field, and having chosen the spot, they returned. Manabus soon
found their tracks and followed them to the place of vantage which they
had selected. He judged by its appearance that they had decided to
stay there, so he concluded that he would not be far away when the game
commenced. Early next morning, before daybreak, he went to the place,
and, through his magic power he changed himself into a tall pine tree,
burnt on one side. At dawn, he heard a great hubbub and whooping.
From everywhere he heard derisive voices calling, "Hau! Hau! Hau!" and
"Hoo! Hoo! Hoo!" to urge on the enemy. Then appeared the deer, the
mink, the otters, and all the land beings and the fishes in human form.
They arrived at their side of the field and took their places and all
became silent for a time. Suddenly the sky grew dark, and the rush of
many wings made a thunderous rumbling, above which rose whoops,
screams, screeches, cackling, calling, hooting, all in one terrific babble.

Then the thunderers swooped down, and the golden eagles, and the
bald eagles, and the buzzards, hawks, owls, pigeons, geese, ducks, and all
manner of birds, and took the opposite end of the field.

Then silence dropped down once more, and the sides lined up, the
weakest near the goals, the strongest in the center. Someone tossed
the ball high in the air and a pell mell melee followed, with deafening
howling and whoopings. Back and forth surged the players, now one
side gaining, now the other. At last one party wrested the ball through
the others' ranks and sped it toward the Chicago goal. Down the field
it went, and Manabus strained his eyes to follow its course. It was nearly
at the goal, and the keepers were rushing to guard it. In the midst of
the brandished clubs, legs, arms, and clouds of dust something notable
was happening that Manabus could not see. In his excitement he forgot
where he was and changed back into a man. Once in human shape he
came to himself, and, looking about, noted that the onlookers had not
yet discovered him. Fired by his lust for revenge, he promptly took his
bow, which he had kept with him all the time, strung it and fired twice at
each of the underground gods, as they sat on their mountain. His arrows

sped true, and the gods rushed for the water, falling all over themselves as they scurried down the hill. The impact of their diving caused great waves to roll down the lake toward the Chicago goal. Some of the players saw them coming, rolling high over the tree tops. "Manabus, Manabus!" They cried in breathless fright.

At once all the players on both sides rushed back to the centerfield to look. "What is the matter?" said everyone to everyone else. "Why, it must have been Manabus. He's done this—nobody else would dare to attack the underground gods." When the excited players reached the center of the field they found that the culprit had vanished. "Let's all look for Manabus," cried someone. "We will use the power of the water for our guide." So the players all waded into the water, and the water rose up and went ahead of them. It knew very well where Manabus had gone.

In the meantime Manabus was skipping away as fast as he could, for he was frightened at what the consequences of his rashness might be. All at once he happened to look back and saw the water flowing after him. He ran faster and faster, but still it came. He doubled, he zigzagged, he dodged, but still it came. He strained himself to his utmost speed and it gained on him. On, on, led the chase, further, and further away.

Source: *Alanson Skinner and John V. Satterlee,* Menomini Folklore, *Anthropological Papers of the Museum of American History 13, part 3 (1913): 255–57.*

This fanciful story is clearly one Menominee version of the "great game" between the birds and land animals, which we have already seen in a Cherokee version (chapter 1), and there may have been other versions (of other tribes or even Menominee) that escaped collecting. The Menominee story is missing the Cherokee episode of creating the bat and flying squirrel to help the birds win—the main point of the North Carolina tale.

Manabus, the Menominee culture hero, is the equivalent of Wenaboozho, the central figure in the next legend. Like Wenaboozho, who can turn himself into a caribou, Manabus is also capable of changing form, in this case into a pine tree for disguise. In this story, all the creatures of the universe change into human beings to play lacrosse—something that does not happen in the Cherokee version of this epic struggle.

Once Manabus begins firing his magic arrows at the gods of the underworld, it is clear whose side he is taking. To understand this, one needs some background. In Indian beliefs the universe is divided into good and bad represented by above (good) and below (bad), much as Christians distinguish between heaven and hell. Thus the sky creatures who dwell in the heavens are the benevolent ones, the underground deities the evil ones.

It is not explained here why Manabus wishes to "take revenge" on the underground spirits, but it is probably explained in some other legend familiar to the listeners. Possibly he is angered he hasn't been invited to watch the game, so must attend it in disguise.

It might seem startling to see the cities of Chicago and Detroit represented as goal locations in an Indian legend. Many Indian storytellers changed minor details of old stories to bring past events more into the present—to provide them a measure of reality for the listeners. It doesn't really matter to the story where the goals were located, and one suspects the storyteller came upon the choice of these two cities on the spot—he might just as easily have selected San Francisco and New York. Although the actual locations of the goals is irrelevant here, Chicago and Detroit are roughly east and west of each other and almost at the same latitude. This would conform to the traditional orientation of the Menominee lacrosse field on an east-west axis, but suggesting Sturgeon Bay then to lie at centerfield is difficult to comprehend. Directly north of Chicago, the Sturgeon Bay area of Wisconsin was at one time part of Menominee territory, so it would have been familiar to the narrator's audience and lent a certain tribal identity to the tale. Also well known are the big waves on Lake Michigan on the shores of "The Windy City." In this story the waves are caused by the gods falling all over themselves, scrambling into the water to escape being shot by Manabus.

There is no question that Manabus is on the side of the thunderers. Turning into a tall pine tree burnt on the one side suggests he has been struck (blessed, maybe) by lightning. Lightning, of course, has strong upper-world connotations. Another Menominee legend explains that when lightning strikes a tree it leaves behind its black marks to guide the stick maker to cut the wood in crafting the lacrosse stick.

Nearly all the details of the game follow what we know of traditional Indian lacrosse, from the taunting yells and war whoops designed to intimidate foes to the toss-up of the ball. The wonderfully descriptive talents of the storyteller bring all the details to life: the various sights and sounds of the challengers arriving, their screeching and flapping wings, and the frantic scrimmage at the goal when a score is threatening—clubs brandished between arms and legs raising a cloud of dust. Lacrosse imagery continues in the story when Manabus is running away, pursued by the waves. He follows the running techniques he has seen in the lacrosse game: he doubles, zigzags, and dodges.

TEAMS AND LACROSSE POSITIONS

This is one of the few legends to touch on actual positions of play in the Indian lacrosse game. The animals "took their places" and the sides lined up, "the weakest near the goal, the strongest in the center." The game in this legend is played by all creatures equally divided according to where their homes are.

From all accounts, traditional games were organized by social units, beginning with nations (tribes), then at the village or community level, then by clan membership, and so on. Even the earliest sources verify this practice. In 1636 the Jesuit Paul le Jeune described the Huron lacrosse season as one village pitted against another. The Creek nation was organized into towns with red or white designations as identification markers. Red towns carried on warfare, whereas white towns were charged with maintaining peace. A similar two-fold division was used by the Ho-Chunk; that division operated on the warpath, at the Chief Feast, and in ceremonial lacrosse games, such as we saw between the Manegi and Wangeregi.

There was little contact between the Creek towns except for lacrosse games. By the late 1930s the color terms were no longer used for identification, although one still referred to another town as "my friend" or "my opponent" or "enemy," and the games were still organized along these lines. Most Creek village games ended peacefully, but often interfamily or interclan squabbles would surface, and games could be staged as grudge matches. One historical photograph from the 1930s shows Creek players circling a goalpost. The photo was discovered by a member of the Creek Nation in an archive, who penciled on the back of the photograph his interpretation of what it represented: "grudge battle fought against clans or families until stopped by government."

Clan systems promoted kinship loyalties and played a strong role in warfare and games, organizing participants according to their affiliations. Onondaga players in late May still divide according to the affiliation with either the Mudhouse or the Longhouse for games. The numbers on each side are unimportant, for, as the Iroquois say, they are "playing for the Creator"; they simply play to three goals. The Cherokee organized lacrosse at the community level. Games between Chicamunga and Chatooga around 1920 had 50 players on each side.

Where tribes are scattered geographically but still united linguistically and culturally, competition could be among the various reservations where tribal members were forcibly settled by the U.S. government in treaties. Thus we find games between traditional rivals, the Bad River and Red Cliff Ojibwe Reservations 30 miles apart but both bordering Lake Superior. Or in the 1880s Rainy Lake Canadian Ojibwe playing Nett Lake Minnesota Ojibwe. Despite the international boundary there are strong familial ties between the two groups, and Nett Lakers traditionally welcomed Rainy Lakers as "guest harvesters" during a wild-rice-picking in the early fall. It is conceivable the two communities played each other in off hours, just as they took part in informal social dancing.

Aside from these social units, how were the players selected? The Creek "Big Warriors" of each town arranged the games. Aside from their civic responsibilities—the power to declare war and punish those breaking council rules or failing to attend the annual harvest festival—they would determine together with Big Warriors of other towns the eligibility of certain players. In question were town members living elsewhere or others who had married into the town. If they could reach no agreement, the game would be called off. The Choctaw had a local leader called Miko (from *micco*, "chief" in Creek) who resolved questions of community affiliation when two teams claimed the same player. The Miko also addressed problems of illegal player recruitment and unfair training practices.

Once all eligible players were determined, how was it decided for which team they would play? When a Great Lakes Indian game had been decided on, the opposing sides would each select a captain who in turn would pick his players. There were some unusual procedures in the decision. When a Menominee game was played as a dream obligation, the dream recipient would choose the two captains. Then, as each player arrived at the field, he would add his stick to the pile. Wooden sticks usually had the owner's personal identification marks on it, such as the four scarcely visible incisions on the underside of an Ojibwe stick, possibly the oldest in existence. In lacrosse of the Potawatomi, one of the captains was blindfolded to draw from the pile; he made up the two teams, with five to nine players per side. The neighboring Menominee followed a similar practice in the early twentieth century. The jumbled sticks were dumped out into two equal rows parallel to each other. The Menominee believed the thunder spirits determined which side a player was on, so, uncomplaining, a player joined the side where his stick had fallen. It is not recorded how teams were chosen among the Bungi (Plains Ojibwe), who played their games on horseback!

TEAM SIZE

What factors determined team size? Evidence suggests that in early games teams were large. If the explorer Jonathan Carver can be believed, games in the Great Lakes area during his period of travel (1766–68) could have as many as 300 playing, particularly if they were "great games" between na-tions, intended to settle territorial disputes and avoid open warfare. Mo-hawks researching the history of their own game believe there may have been as many as 100 per team. Over time, factors such as warfare with Europeans, population reductions, and intertribal divisions affected team size; the researchers see the formerly massive game begin to disappear in favor of spe-cialized positions and team strategy. Still, by the end of the eighteenth cen-tury, large numbers of players were still being reported on Iroquois fields. In the 1797 game between Seneca and Mohawk, "platoons" of 60 new players were exchanged after every 20 minutes of play.

Cherokee lacrosse rules required that the two teams be at equal strength at all times. Before every game, players lined up at midfield to lay down their sticks pointing to their opposing numbers. During this match-up, game directors walked back and forth making adjustments to players' weights, heights, and sizes, trying to arrive at even matches. If an injured player re-tired from the game, his opposite number had to leave as well. Cherokee play-ers could withdraw voluntarily from a lacrosse match if they had "had enough"—a practice paralleling the voluntary departure from a war party at any time to head home. The equal-number principle tended to discourage the practice of "double teaming," when two players would gang up on the same opponent. This maneuver always risked leaving one player unguarded from the other team and free to score. The voluntary withdrawals from a game could lead to drastic reductions in the team size. In the 1930s, Lloyd Se-quoyah, playing against Yellow Hill (one of the communities on the Qualla/ Eastern Cherokee Reservation) scored the winning goal for Big Cove (the most conservative and traditional of the Qualla communities) as the sole remaining player!

Ritual games often prescribed a specific number of players. There were seven players per side to represent the seven thunder gods of the Cayuga. The seven older men from one tribal division played seven younger from the opposite division—the game being conceived of as fathers competing against sons.

POSITIONS

As team size decreased, there was an increased emphasis on position skills. The Menominee legend states that the strongest players were put at center field, the weaker near the goal. Similarly, the Cherokee developed the position of "center fighter." Formerly they had two center fighters but eventually reduced the position to one. The biggest, strongest, and tallest player always held this position, as he had to compete in toss-ups at midfield. His size and reach were crucial in snatching the ball in midair on its descent. He came to be called "shortstop" or "center knocker" and eventually served as a team captain. By the 1940s this captain would select 20 players, although there were only 12 at a time per team to play in the customary three games each summer. At the toss-up, the center fighter would hold his sticks together over his right shoulder like a baseball batter or hold his sticks outstretched behind him and to one side; he was prepared to leap toward the ball on its descent, trying to jump up with his sticks together and bat the ball to a teammate (thus the name "knocker" for this position) (see plate 3).

Sources are vague at best in describing any sort of defenseman. Early reports such as the one on the Huron imply a kind of zone defense. Typically, there was a sort of phalanx defense of the ball carrier; whenever a player was about to score, his teammates would surround him to keep the opposition at bay. This may have been what George Beers complained about in the Mohawk game, a practice he called "bunching" near the goal, to which he attributed many injuries. Lewis H. Morgan, one of the few sources on the historical Iroquois lacrosse, suggests one means of preventing the ball carrier from scoring: some players would detach themselves from the group around the ball and take up positions on a diagonal line to intercept the runner should he get the ball.

Mohawk Indian researchers have suggested the probable evolution of the position of goaltender. Formerly, if a goal were threatened, the tendency was to put all defenders to block scoring, like a human wall of soccer players facing a penalty kick. Then they began to train one or two players to specialize in blocking shots—this they see as the birth of the goaltender. Once Mohawk teams began playing Canadians after about 1850, there had to be a greater emphasis on team playing in specialized positions and strategy. Many older Indian players consistently expressed preference for the older style of play, which allowed the individual a better chance to show off his talents.

Because the older sticks lacked guard strings or a true pocket, the contest had to have been characterized more as a running than a passing game. The slightest jarring would cause a ball carrier to drop the ball so carefully balanced on his webbing.

Players became renowned for certain skills: Franklin Basina, a Red Cliff Ojibwe, heaped praise on his former teammates, the Bear brothers, who were adept at catching. "It's the Bear boys, Bobby Bear, Simon Bear, and all them. They were the guys that it gets the ball in flight, just like capture, an outfielder would do, put that stick out, and that God damn ball would be right in the pocket!"*

Although team play increased at the expense of individualism, players were still noted for their style of play and given nicknames to describe it, such as the Choctaw names emphasizing keen eyesight or escaping skills:

palki (fast player)
sala'na wasona (slow player)
siti (snake)
canasa (moccasin snake)
opa niskin (owl eyes)

Why the Turkey Buzzard Has a Red Scabby Neck (Ojibwe)

Wenaboozho, the trickster figure of the Menominee's western neighbors, the Ojibwe, is the nearly exact counterpart of Manabus in all his dimensions, and many of the episodes in their two careers are identical. The tribes are both Algonquian-speakers and shared many cultural similarities—the medicine lodge, the Big Drum ceremony, and styles of hunting, trapping, and wigwam

*Franklin Basina, interview by Thomas Vennum, Lacrosse Transcripts, Archives of the Center for Folklife and Cultural Studies, Smithsonian Institution, Washington, DC.

The following is a representational list of plants that played a role as "medicines" in preparing Eastern Cherokee ballplayers for a game. The medicine was usually made by boiling in water some or all of the plant, sometimes with other ingredients. The decoction was either drunk or applied to the body and limbs of the player usually after he had undergone the scratching ritual. Raymond Fogelson compiled these from several sources, noting that his list was by no means exhaustive. Some of the plants were identified for him by a naturalist.

Common Name	Latin Name	Effect
Beggar lice, or wild confrey	*Cynoglossum virginianum*	Roots are shaped like human beings, they are given names of opposing players and burned in the fire to bring them harm.
Black raspberry	*Rubus occidentalis*	Stem has briars; by chewing the root, one never misses a tackle.
Black walnut	*Juglans nigra*	Bark is used for dyeing feathers worn in a player's hair; a decoction of roots or bark is used to prevent cramps.
Bloodroot	*Sanguinaria canadensis*	Dye for feathers.
Bulrush	*Scirpus validus*	When trodden, the stalk snaps back up; players will recover if knocked on the ground.
Butterfly root	*Asclepias tuberosa*	Dye for feathers.
Common rush (wire grass, hemp rush)	*Juncus tenuis*	Decoction of whole plant; trodden, its stem snaps back in place; players will recover if knocked over.
Crabapple (wild)	*Pyrus malus*	Used together with decoction of vicia and pine needles; will prevent player's trunk from hitting the ground if tackled.
Crown vetch	*Coronilla varia*	Bathing and decoction; keeps player from injury.
Devil's shoestring	?	Prevents short-windedness; increases stamina.

Common Name	Latin Name	Effect
Fetterbask (dog hobble, drooping lencothoe, "Hemlock Bush")	*Leucothoe editorum*	Prevents cramps.
Goat's rue (catgut, devil's shoestrings, turkey or rabbit pea)	*Tephrosia virginiana*	Toughens limbs and hardens muscles.
Great rhododendron	*Rhododendron maximum*	Leaves worn in players' hair as ornaments.
Hawthorne	*Crataegus macrosperma*	Wards off tacklers; sharp thorns discourage opponents from grabbing.
Hickory	*Carya sp.*	Toughens players; prevents injury from falling on ground.
Honey locust	*Gleditsia triacanthos*	Wards off tacklers; a thorny tree, no one wants to run into it.
Ironwood	*Carpinus carolinianus*	Prevents injuries from tackles.
Knife blade	?	Its sticky properties helps a player hold on to his sticks and to grab opponents.
Mountain laurel	*Kalonia latifola*	Prevents cramps.
Oldfield cinquefoil	*Potentilla canadensis*	Rubbed on legs, provides protection from "rabbit soup" secretly poured on pathway to the field.
Old tobacco	*Nicotiana rustica*	Burned in the sacred fire during a ball-game dance to scare away evil spirits.
Pitch pine (jack table, or mountain pine)	*Pinus virginiana*	Switching with charred limbs burned in ball-game fire keeps player fresh, always going.
Pussy-toes	*Antennaria plantaginifolia*	Prevents cramps.
Slippery elm (red elm)	*Ulmus rubra muhl*	Bark is chewed, spittle rubbed on the body to make slippery, prevent opponents from grasping.

continued

Common Name	Latin Name	Effect
Sassafras	*Sassafras albidum*	Root chewed before a game for long-windedness, loosening of the "frame."
Saw brier	*Similax glauca*	Like "rabbit soup," sprinkled on opponents' path to the field to weaken them.
Small-leafed briar (sensitive briar)	*Schrankia microphylla*	Plant has "claws" that can grab or trip person; in a decoction with other ingredients, when spilled between the enemies "home sticks," it will knock them off their feet.
Star grass	*Hypoxia hirsuta*	Makes bodies supple.
Tearthumb	*Polygonum sagittatum*	Because the plant has stickers on it, nothing gets away from a player.
Timber willow (mountain willow)	*Salix hamilis*	Gives a player extra wind; "loosens 'the frame.'"
Trumpet weed (Queen of the Meadow, blow-gun weed, Joe-Pye weed)	*Eupatorium purpureum*	Stem used for a drinking straw.
Vetch	*Vicia caroliniana*	Increased wind and toughened muscles.
Wild pea (Partridge pea)	*Casssia nictitans/ Cassia fasciculata*	Prevents fatigue.
Yellow root	*Xanthorhiza simplicissima*	Dye for feathers.

Source: *Raymond Fogelson, "The Cherokee Ballgame: A Study in Southeastern Ethnology" (Ph.D. diss., University of Pennsylvania, 1962), Appendix B.*

and canoe construction. Living in the same environment, the Ojibwe followed the same seasonal cycle as the Menominee; they were settled in villages on rivers and lakes in the summer months, where they fished and gardened. After the wild rice harvest in the late summer, they departed to their winter hunting grounds; with the arrival of spring, when warm days and cold nights began the flow of sap in the maple trees, they moved out to their "sugarbush" camps to make maple sugar.

Robert Ritzenthaler, who collected this legend, received his doctorate in anthropology from Columbia University in 1950. Having studied the culture of the Oneida Indians in upstate New York, he shifted his interest to the cultures of Great Lakes peoples. He and his wife Pat co-authored publications on Wisconsin Indian tribes, and Ritzenthaler directed the research of anthropology students in northern Wisconsin, where he was in charge of purchasing ethnographic specimens for the Milwaukee Public Museum. Among his valuable contributions was the documentation in film and a monograph on Ojibwe birch-bark canoe construction on the Lac du Flambeau Reservation, focusing on master craftsman Bob Pine. That reservation was the source of "Wakayabide Is Killed Playing Lacrosse and Later Takes Revenge" (chapter 3), collected by Ritzenthaler's student Victor Barnouw.

Once, Wenaboozho turned himself into a caribou and laid down, pretending he was dead. All fall and winter, birds and animals came and ate from his carcass. But the turkey buzzard knew that Wenaboozho was a spirit, so he stayed up in a tree watching until just the bones were left and not much meat. He thought, "It's safe. Wenaboozho surely must be dead by now," so he flew down to feast, but the only meat that was left was around the anus. He started eating that until his head was completely inside. Then Wenaboozho tightened his anus, catching the head of the turkey buzzard inside. Then he got up, the turkey buzzard still clamped to his bottom, and walked to a nearby village where the Indians were playing lacrosse. He asked if he could get in the game, and they said, "Sure." At one point while Wenaboozho was playing, he tripped and fell, and the turkey buzzard slipped out and got away. But in escaping, his head and neck were badly scraped, so that is why the buzzard has a red and scabby neck today. He also smells because of that.

Source: *Robert Ritzhenthaler, field notes and papers, Anthropology Section, Milwaukee Public Museum, s.v. "Myths."*

The Ojibwe turkey buzzard story, another etiological tale, was invented to explain to children why, when almost all other birds have feathers on their heads and necks, the turkey buzzard doesn't. Instead, he has an ugly, raw, knobby, sore-looking head. At some point in the Ojibwe distant past, some child must have asked his elders why this was so, and the story, however fanciful, was created, and the trickster Wenaboozho was a logical culprit to lay the blame to. Also, anyone who has gotten close to a turkey buzzard knows how badly this bird stinks from feasting on dead and rotting flesh. Incidentally, the story also offers a clever explanation that prudish people outside of Ojibwe culture might find offensive. But children the world over are certainly aware of the unpleasant odor of human and animal waste. Buzzards and other "cleanup" creatures are accustomed to devouring every bit of the carcass they fight over, with little regard to its bodily function when the creature was alive. American Indian children, traditionally closer to nature in daily life than their more comfortable Euro-American counterparts, were far less squeamish about such matters. They were never taught that anything to do with excreting waste was a taboo topic.

Variations of this story are told by other tribes, although without the lacrosse connection. The Ho-Chunk trickster plays dead as a buck-deer, not a caribou, to capture the head of Hawk, as punishment for Hawk having played a trick on him. In some versions, it is the trickster who is captured, like the turkey buzzard. Sitcombi, the trickster-hero of the Assiniboine Indians in Manitoba, is tempted to put his head into a buffalo skull in which mice are dancing; then his head is trapped. In another version, flies inside an elk's skull instruct the trickster how to command the elk's neck to enlarge, allowing him to put his head inside. The flies then run away, and the neck opening tightens, trapping his head.

ATHLETIC DRESS IN INDIAN LACROSSE

Given the plot of Wenaboozho's predicament, one can well imagine the curious child asking the storyteller, "But if he's got a turkey vulture hanging out his butt, why would they take him for just another Indian ready to play lacrosse? He must have looked really weird!"

Wenaboozho's ready acceptance by the other lacrosse players despite his unusual appearance can be explained by examining the sort of athletic dress players customarily wore onto the field. With the turkey buzzard's head and neck tightly clamped inside his buttocks, Wenaboozho asks the village Indians if he can play; he is semi-naked except for the remainder of the bird with all its feathers in a clump, looking probably like a feather duster. A player today would never consider such an outrageous costume to wear onto the field, but this collection of feathers above his buttocks would not have been an unusual ornament for a lacrosse player of some tribes.

Athletic dress for Indian players in many places seems to have been a matter of personal preference. Because athletes needed to be "stripped for action," it is doubtful that players would have worn the ceremonial beadwork depicted in paintings and photos of players in northern Wisconsin (plate 7). This would not only have been cumbersome, but also risked damage. Still, Indian lacrosse players traditionally adorned themselves with a wide variety of ceremonial tailpieces, including feather bustles. Any number of materials might have been used to make up that tailpiece. Among southeastern tribes, players wore an elaborate rear ornament designed combining cloth, wood, and hair probably from the horse's mane or tail. As noted earlier, George Catlin, painting at Fort Gibson in Indian Territory (present-day Oklahoma) in 1834, showed the elaborate Choctaw version of this tailpiece as being worn by every one of the nearly hundred players he depicted on the field. It is not certain how accurately he painted what he saw. Given the rough and tumble nature of Choctaw ball play, it is strange that in his depiction of these fairly flimsy tail pieces, not one is shown as askew, broken, bent, or even knocked off onto the ground. Contemporary members of the Choctaw tribe have continued the practice of the ornamental tailpiece well into the twentieth century (see plate 8).

Catlin's portraits of players from other tribes show them wearing other types of tailpieces. His painting of "Ah-no-je-nahge"—titled "He Who Stands on Both Sides, a distinguished ballplayer"—shows him wearing a tailpiece made from what look to be feathers. The subject is an Eastern Dakota Indian from that branch of the Sioux that shared much culture, including their lacrosse game, with the Ojibwe. Frank Mayer's painting of "Ma-kah-mon-oton mahnee" (The Sounding Earth That Walked), also a Dakota, shows a bustle apparently made of dangling animal skins, not feathers. Presbyterian missionary and historian Edward D. Neill described Dakota players in Minnesota as being naked (like Wenaboozho?) except for pieces of decoration— "painted in divers colors, with no article of apparel, with feathers in their hands, bells around their wrists, and fox and wolf tails dangling behind."

Catlin was at Fort Snelling (present-day Minnesota) in 1835 for a Fourth of July demonstration game between southwestern Ojibwe and Dakota Sioux teams, where the players appeared with "ornamented sash, a tail, extending nearly to the ground, made of the choicest arrangement of quills and feathers, or of the hair of white horses' tails" (see figure 11). In a Ho-Chunk trickster legend, Hawk has been trapped in the rectum of the buck-deer pretending to be dead. Bear admires the trickster's tailpiece and wonders how he can get such a nice, ornamental tailpiece for himself. Trickster then relaxes his anus and releases Hawk—like the turkey buzzard, minus some feathers—telling him to go get more feathers for Bear.

VIOLENCE IN THE INDIAN GAME

The turkey buzzard escapes when Wenaboozho takes a hard hit. Anyone involved with lacrosse, particularly those who have played it, know what a physical game it is. The fact that American Indians used it as a proving ground for young warriors says much about equating fighting skills on the playing field with those needed in combat. Over the years, however, considerable myths about Indian lacrosse have been accepted. The most common image has hundreds on the field, playing days at a time, roaming over enormous areas and leaving dead and injured players behind.

There *was* violence in the Indian game, but it needs to be put in some perspective. The nonnative myth can be traced to a number of sources, beginning with the notion of "the noble savage," an image put forth by European romantics in the nineteenth century. George Catlin's paintings of Choctaw players in 1834 did much to perpetuate this image. Painting on the frontier in Indian Territory, Catlin deliberately exaggerated for effect in many of his pictures. He wanted to convey to viewers back East and in Europe the great excitement he felt watching this Indian sport; if he needed to put 100 players on the field to give this impression instead of the 50 he probably saw, there was no one around to question his accuracy.

Many European travelers and fur traders in North America were horrified at the violence they witnessed in Indian ball games and never failed to mention it in their published accounts. They were accustomed, of course, to milder European sports, which were well regulated and played in gentlemanly fashion. French Baron de Lahotan (1666–1715) visiting the Huron Indians in Georgian Bay in 1700 wrote, "This game is so violent they tear their skins and break their legs very often." A century later, farther west, trader Peter Grant (1764–1848) described rematches of the Saulteaux north of Lake Superior, where players let nothing get in their way, knocking over and trampling opponents underfoot. He described the field as covered with players sprawled out "with wounded legs and broken heads."

One part of the Indian anatomy subject to punishment was the collarbone. In the Cayuga game, where slashing was also permitted as long as a player had both hands on the stick, a player could lift an opponent off the ground and dump him, often fracturing his collarbone. When Cherokee players were tossed into the air, to protect themselves they would instinctively hold the head to one side and extend one arm; often this maneuver resulted in a broken collarbone.

Not until Indians began playing against Canadians in the nineteenth century did they begin to wear protective gear; as there was no equipment expressly designed for lacrosse, they adopted baseball and hockey gear. Before that period, it was customary to be "stripped for action," wearing minimal clothing, which might otherwise slow the player down or provide an opponent something to grab onto. (Preparing for a game, Cherokee players would rub their bodies with "slippery eel" to prevent opponents from holding on to them.) Because mostly they played in their bare feet and wore only a breechcloth, injuries were commonplace. The Iroquois had been used to playing with a lightweight, small stuffed deerskin ball before they adopted the hard India-rubber ball, which could inflict considerable damage. Onondaga elder Oren Lyons, current coach of the Iroquois Nationals, playing goalie as a teenager (figure 12), was once severely injured by a "heavy shot" from Mohawk Angus Thomas, a legendary St. Regis defenseman. Fellow Mohawk, Frank Benedict, described Thomas's powerful shot: "He had one of the hardest shots in the league. He'd hit a goaltender, and he'd be pushed back behind the goal line." Thomas's shot broke three of Lyons's ribs; because there was no backup goalie, he was forced to finish the game. Later in life, Thomas retired from the game, having accidentally killed a player. Even into the twentieth century, some native players preferred playing without protective gear. In British Columbia, New Salmonbellies goalie Henry "Hawkeye" Baker wore no goalie pads at all.

As dangerous as the hard-rubber ball was the wooden lacrosse ball traditionally used in the Great Lakes region. It was carved from a pine knot, which meant the wood fibers were packed with concentrated resin, making the ball

FIGURE 12.
Onondaga goalie Oren Lyons, circa 1930. Note minimal protective gear, football shoulder pads and jersey, and hockey gloves.

Photo courtesy Roy Simmons Jr.

heavy and hard. Players hit in the head with it were usually knocked unconscious. Bad River Ojibwe Leonard Marksman was knocked down by such a ball in a 1948 game and stunned for 10 minutes. The Great Lakes special "whistling" ball with the hole drilled through it, as it came careening through the air gave out a hair-raising screech, which at least provided some warning.

Rarely do we read of restrictions against intentional injuries in Indian lacrosse. All kinds of behavior were allowed, which in today's field game are infractions incurring penalties. Slashing with a stick, tripping, stabbing with the butt end of the stick, charging, fist-fighting, grabbing from behind and holding, tackling an opponent to wrestle him to the ground—these and similar actions characterized Indian players' performance, especially in the Cherokee game.

There were some situations in Indian lacrosse expressly permitting violent action. In Ojibwe lacrosse, if a player you were pursuing was "hogging" the ball and not passing it, his opponent could yell "*bagadoon* [throw it, get rid of it]." If he still cradled the ball, after the pursuer yelled the command three times, he was permitted to smash the ball carrier's head from behind with his stick. Formerly, choking was another action condoned, especially by the Cherokee. Given the small size of the ball, a player might try to carry it concealed in his mouth rather than between his rackets, but in doing so he risked being choked to spit it out. But just as these particular aggressive moves were permitted, elsewhere there were at least a few specific infractions. Head-butting was expressly outlawed in the mid-nineteenth-century Choctaw game, for example. If it happened, a five-goal penalty was assessed against the offending player's team.

With so much violence on the field, it is not surprising to read reports of Indian games that dissolved into free-for-alls. Seneca oral history tells of their people driving the Erie Indians (a northern Iroquoian tribe) from western New York in a 1654 war. The fighting started out as a "breach of faith or treachery" in a lacrosse game the Erie had challenged the Seneca to play. Mississippi Choctaw recalled games in the past when there were so many injuries the game had to be called. In a 1947 Cherokee game, six players were hospitalized within the first 15 minutes of play. Basil Hall in 1827 relates how while he had been watching Creek Indians play lacrosse, the Indian agent recommended he leave before the end of the game, when players would customarily start attacking each other with their sticks.

Sports historian Kendall Blanchard, an authority on Choctaw stickball, writes of an early twentieth-century game in which a fight broke out at the first toss-up. The fight lasted three hours; although county sheriffs and deputies were brought in, they failed to stop it. (Bringing in the local constabulary to restore order was not restricted to native games. In the 1960 Mann Cup semi-finals in British Columbia, when the New Westminster fans began fighting locals, the Royal Canadian Mounted Police had to be called.)

Native doctors on the sidelines would treat most minor injuries for the Cherokees. An injured player could take himself out of the game, but because it was vital to have exactly the same number on each side at all times, his opponent was expected to retire from the game as well. Even before a game, however, the Cherokee medicine man, functioning as a sort of coach, by consulting his magic beads was able to weed out weak players who might otherwise get hurt (see figure 1). He also had protective prayers he could recite from the sidelines to protect his players, as well as magic formulas to expose opponents to injury.

By the time the Indian game became "more civilized," particularly once Indians began playing white teams and wearing protective equipment, according to the "old-timers" the game had lost its spark and life, and the young players of the day seemed to them to be unable to take the punishment they remembered from their own youth.

5

Trees to Stop the Action

If Wenaboozho's tailpiece seems an unusual mode of athletic dress and Red Horn's human head earrings are enough to rattle his opponent, imagine coming on the field to find the other team with live poisonous serpents draped over them!

This happens in a long Eastern Cherokee legend about a great gambler named Untsaya, who, whenever he loses, changes into the form of some animal and thereby makes his escape. The lacrosse episode is used to demonstrate the bravery of a young man in his travels and once again shows the close relationship between lacrosse and warfare. James Mooney (see chapter 1) collected this legend from his principal informant, Swimmer, as well as from John Ax (b. 1800). He had the story confirmed by James Wafford, an Oklahoma Cherokee.

Snakes around the Neck (Cherokee)

A young man born in the East and said to be a son of Thunder, from birth has been afflicted with scrofula sores, which cover his body. [Scrofula is a disease of the lymph glands resulting in skin eruptions.] He journeys to seek a father who can cure him, who has the son boiled with certain roots and thrown into a river to treat him. When his wife retrieves the boy from the water, he has miraculously been cured of scrofula, and his skin is clear.

On the way home the wife tells the boy, "When we go in, your father will put new clothes on you, but when he opens his box and tells you to pick out your ornaments, be sure to take them from the bottom. Then he will send for his other sons to play lacrosse against you. There is a honey-locust tree in front of the house, and as soon as you begin to get tired, aim your blows at that and your father will stop the play, because he does not want to lose the tree."

When they went into the house, the old man was pleased to see the boy looking so clean, and said, "I knew I could soon cure those spots. Now we must dress you." He brought out a fine suit of buckskin, with a belt and headdress, and had the boy put them on. Then he opened a box and said, "Now pick out your necklace and bracelets." The boy looked, and the box was full of all kinds of snakes gliding over each other with their heads up. He was not afraid, but remembered what the woman had told him and plunged his hand to the bottom and took out a large rattlesnake and put it around his neck for a necklace. Then he put down his hand again four times and drew up four copperheads, which he twisted around his wrists and ankles. Then his father gave him a war club and said, "Now you must play a ball-game with your two elder brothers. They live beyond here in 'the Darkening Land' and I have sent for them." He said a ball-game, but he meant that the boy must fight for his life. The young men came, and they were both older and stronger than the boy, but he was not afraid and fought against them. The thunder rolled and the lightning flashed at every stroke, for they were the young Thunders, and the boy himself was Lightning. At last he was tired from defending himself against the two and pretended to aim a blow at the honey-locust tree. Then his father stopped the fight because he was afraid the lightning would split the tree, and he had already seen that the boy was brave and strong.

Source: *James Mooney, "Myths of the Cherokee,"* 19th Annual Report of the Bureau of American Ethnology, *part 1 (Washington, DC: Government Printing Office, 1900), 311–15.*

This legend is explicit in equating lacrosse with fighting a battle—an underlying theme we have seen repeatedly: "[The father] said a ball-game but he meant that the boy must fight for his life," so he provides his son with a "[war] club," meaning a lacrosse stick. Ridding the boy of his skin sores can be taken as the equivalent of training lacrosse players to be in perfect shape for games. The Creek like the Cherokee bathed themselves with certain protective [curative] herbs before a game. (The healing and magical effects of water play their role in Indian lacrosse.) Like the Cherokee medicine man who "takes his players to water," the son in this legend is thrown in the river.

By casting the three combatants in roles as Thunderers, the legend attributes supernatural powers to them, so that the game is characterized by violent thunder and lightning, which the thunder spirits control. The violence is such that the father fears his tree is in danger of destruction by the son who is the personification of Lightning.

ORNAMENTS IN INDIAN LACROSSE DRESS

The story focuses on what the young man will wear in preparation for "battle." To dress him, the father gives him a new buckskin suit with a belt and headdress, more suggestive of ceremonial than military attire. Such items are considerably more lavish than anything the Cherokee or others normally wore during lacrosse games. Game wear was often as minimal as what men wore confronting an enemy. The belt possibly refers to the special decorative belt of other southeastern players like the Choctaw. The headdress, however, suggests the stereotypical warbonnet of Plains Indians, which would rarely have been worn in a game. A few photographs from the nineteenth century show Indian players wearing warbonnets, but invariably these players were "costumed" for exhibition games and posed for team photographs (see plate 7), particularly in Europe, where the spectators expected them to look "Indian." Often these Indian teams would follow their exhibition game with "a war dance," also conforming to the stereotyped impressions of Native Americans. A typical exhibition lacrosse match was the appearance in 1867 of a Six Nations Canadian team in a game before a baseball tournament in Troy, New York, whose "colorful" Indian players wore a variety of headdresses and brightly colored tights. Another headpiece clearly "for show" and sometimes depicted on Indian lacrosse players is the bristly "roach," made of porcupine guard hairs and deer tails. Today, this style of headdress frequently makes its appearance in the commercial exploitation of the nineteenth century concept of the "noble savage" image—in the late twentieth century, on commercially marketed T-shirts and in lacrosse equipment advertisements. In a team photograph of 12 Caughnawaga Mohawk traveling to England in 1876 with the Montreal Lacrosse club for exhibition matches, the players wear horizontally striped jerseys over long underwear; and for footwear they have on leather booties. In the group photo only the captain, Chief Big John, wears a feather headdress—surely to identify his role but also possibly to demonstrate his pride in Indian identification.

The snake ornaments deserve comment. As if it were not enough for the boy in the Cherokee legend to have lightning bolts in his armory, by donning these poisonous serpents he would have intended to acquire some of their attributes through sympathetic magic. Just as Creek players or warriors wore "tiger tails" to gain the ferocity of that animal, Cherokee players attached pieces of bat's wing to their sticks in the belief that the bat's darting ability, featured in the legend of the game between the birds and animals (chapter 1), would be transferred to the player in the game. Similarly, the addition of snakes around the neck, wrists, and ankles would impart to the player the abilities of the snakes to make quick strikes (with lightning speed), or to slither out of an opponent's grasp, or to elude him by running in a zigzag fashion.

The powers of snakes were invoked in ritual formulas (prayers) recited by a Cherokee conjurer, such as the one to "the Red Rattlesnake." Although later these were supplanted by steel straight pins, rattlesnake fangs were once used to incise the skin in ritual "scratching," as described in chapter 3. In the Southeast, snake rattles were tied into a player's hair and diamond-shaped cross-hatching representing rattlesnakes was carved into or painted on lacrosse sticks as design symbols. Indian lacrosse players in nineteenth-century portraits by George Catlin and sketches by Frank Myers show them adorned with all sorts of feathers and furs. Catlin claimed he painted his players "fresh from a game," complete with bells, not snakes, around their wrists and fox and wolf tails dangling from their belts, called "drops" (see figure 11).

BODY PAINT AND TEAM IDENTIFICATION

In today's sports, the pattern of a uniform's design and its colors provide instant distinction between teams. With the large numbers of players on a large Indian lacrosse field, how were the teams marked? In some cases it appears that body paint was the distinguishing element. Catlin's action paintings of the Choctaw—what James Mooney called "Catlin's spirited ball pictures"—show all of them wearing the special Choctaw tailpiece, so players on both sides have that item of dress in common. Obviously impressed with what he saw, Catlin wrote: "I pronounce such a scene, with its hundreds of Nature's most beautiful models, denuded, and painted of various colours, running and leaping into the air in all the most extravagant and varied forms, in the desperate struggles for the ball, a school for the painter or sculptor equal to any of those which ever inspired the hand of the artist in the Olympian games or the Roman forum . . . It is impossible for pen and ink alone, or brushes . . . to give more than a caricature of such a scene!"*

Despite the challenge, Catlin produced far more than caricatures, and his fabulous, exciting lacrosse paintings are well known among fans of the sport. The artist tried to use different colors to suggest opposing players: in his group action painting of players grappling together, some appear with light-colored skin, others with dark. The same mode of distinguishing was practiced as recently as 1955 by the Mexican Kickapoo in clan games: they used white ashes or charcoal carbon on skin not covered by the loincloth, moccasins, or leggings. Some means of the team identification seem to have been improvised—in northern Wisconsin, for example, Ojibwe teams wore different colored sweat bands around the forehead.

Face paint persists in some Indian lacrosse. Formerly, Creek warriors painted themselves before battle, and some Creek still apply modest designs in red or black as face paint, using designs originating in warfare preparations (see figure 11). But elsewhere this practice was gradually given up. At one time painting one's face with lively, ornamental designs was a common daily practice; it disappeared as Indian people faced the ridicule of whites, calling it "warpaint" and labeling those who practiced it "bucks" or "braves." Only a few tribes in North America continue face painting—Seri (*comca'ac*) women in Sonora, Mexico, for instance. Where the practice has been revived today in ceremonies or games like with the Creek, it is used to express native pride, similar to knotting the red scarf (not snakes) around the neck in touching the roots of their traditional culture.

There is no evidence that Indians ever played lacrosse in the nude, despite depictions of the practice in works of art like an 1853 sculpture by Henry Kirk Brown, showing two naked players in a clutch—a maneuver permitted in the southeastern game. Although he never saw an Indian lacrosse game, Brown

*George Catlin, *Letters and Notes on the Manners, Customs, and Condition of the North American Indians*, 2 vols. (London: Tosswill and Myers, 1841; reprint, Minneapolis: Ross and Haines, 1965), 2:123.

was an early student of anatomy and frequently used Greek models as a source of inspiration. Greek gods appear to have been his models for the sculpture; the only apparel the players wear are fanciful, winged helmets or headpieces, suggesting classical images of Hermes or Mercury. Such efforts seem part of the romantic image of "the noble savage" as a child of nature, avoiding such elements of "civilization" as clothing. Indian athletes certainly had their own standards of modesty, but wrestling nude as in Greek Olympics was not one of their practices.

In the twentieth century, Indian teams began to add further distinguishing markings to identify their affiliation, probably a reflection of increased playing against white teams. The early part of the century saw nonnative lacrosse moving toward identifications not only of teams but also individual players. The 1909 minutes of the Montreal Amateur Athletic Association suggest that a committee be formed to investigate giving players numbers and printing programs for spectators showing a roster of players with their identification numbers. (Ultimately there was a rule change in 1930 requiring 6-inch-high numbers on the backs of jerseys.) By the early twentieth century Indian jerseys were sporting tribal affiliations. A circa 1902 photo shows members of the O[nondaga] lacrosse team; because the letters are sewn to jerseys or white shirts, it suggests the increased frequency of matches with white teams, as does the wearing of tennis shoes. Despite conforming to white standards of dress on the field in competition with Canadian teams, in sacred games traditions maintain. At Six Nations Reserve the Cayuga players are barefoot and stripped to the waist in their midwinter game.

Changes in Indian lacrosse dress over time are recorded for some tribes. These changes document stages of acculturation, as Indian people increasingly adopted the clothing of the dominant society. For the Creek Green Corn Ceremony, players originally wore small animal skins as breechclouts. About 1850 these began to be replaced with red wool cloth using abstract geometric designs made with velvet ribbons. By the 1940s, players wore a tapered V-shaped clout, which has been retained today but is worn over bathing suits or underpants. One finds young players today wearing football jerseys, sneakers, and cut-off jeans with white tube socks. Still, for proud tribal identification, some Creek add the knotted red scarf around the neck. Also stressing their native status in the 1930s, the North Shore Indians of British Columbia wore jerseys, predominantly white with red and blue trim, which featured a large stereotype of an Indian head on the front, a logo that would later be taken up by the professional Blackhawk hockey team.

By the time of Mooney's Eastern Cherokee photographs (1888), players wore white muslin shorts. Appliqué decorations in red and blue were in the form of a star, a cross (talented, but not yet a star), or circles or initials telling a player's town, such as B[ig] C[ove], the most conservative community on the reservation. Mooney's photos show a transitional period; in his team pictures, some still wear breechclouts. Elsewhere the breachclout was abandoned, like the traditional Iroquois *ga-ka* of deerskin or broadcloth, nine inches wide and two yards long, ornamented with bead- or quillwork and held in place by a deerskin belt (see plate 1).

For wintertime play on the ice in the nineteenth century, Minnesota Indians wore everyday warm clothing, loose buckskin-fringed shirts, or hooded capotes (figure 13). Like Greek wrestlers and pankration athletes who kept their hair short, most Indian lacrosse players reduced themselves to the bare essentials (most were barefoot), providing little for an opponent to grab onto. Cherokee breechclouts were deliberately made weak to break in a scuffle.

Many played in their bare feet, although there seems to have been some choice in the matter. Deas's portrait of Dakota players shows some barefoot, others wearing moccasins (see figure 11). Catlin's Choctaw and Dakota lacrosse players from the 1830s are barefoot, as are Mooney's Cherokee players in photographs from the late 1880s. Mexican Kickapoo in the 1950s still wore breechclouts and leggings; they had specially reinforced moccasins to withstand the hard, rocky, Sonoran soil they played on. Weather, however, was apparently not a factor in the choice of footwear. Ojibwe played barefoot on the frozen Rainy River at International Falls on the Canadian border.

Red Horn's earrings, which rattled his opponent when the tiny heads winked their eyes and stuck out their tongues, seem unique to that legend (chapter 4). There is no evidence of any similar jewelry worn by Indian lacrosse players, although Eastern Cherokee sometimes wore rhododendron leaves tied to the hair. But in this legend the player's choice of snakes for wristlets and a necklace underlies the belief in sympathetic magic; whatever the player chose to wear into battle would transfer its powers to him.

An Unusual Penalty Box (Seneca)

The following Seneca legend from present-day upstate New York shows that deliberate, violent play occasionally resulted in a player's ejection from the game.

FIGURE 13.
An 1850 etching after Seth Eastman's painting "Ball Play of the Sioux on the St. Peter's River in Winter" (1848). Note the broken and dropped sticks on the ice and the variety of headdresses and hooded capotes. The items in the lower left foreground may have been goods that were wagered on.

Photo courtesy the Minnesota Historical Society

As they traveled along on their journey they saw that the trees of all kinds were very large and tall, and that they were in full bloom and of surpassing beauty. The travelers were greatly surprised to learn that the flowers supplied the light of that world, and they also observed that all the beasts and animals and birds they encountered possessed exceptionally fine bodies and presence. They remarked, too, that they had seen nothing so far during their journey thither so wonderful and strange. They saw with astonishment also the exuberance of the growing grass and plants, among which they beheld in rich stands the fruit stalks of the strawberry plants, which were as tall as the grasses. During the entire journey thus far never had they found such large, luscious berries.

Having gone a considerable ways into the new country, they were surprised to see in the distance a great multitude of human beings, who were assembled on a heath, which appeared to be the playground of that people; the humans seemed to be occupied with games of amusement. Dehaenyowens, the leader of the band of travelers, said, "What is to be done now, my friends, seeing that we have arrived at the dwelling place of strange human beings, and that we have nothing with which to defend ourselves should they attempt to do us harm?" Thereupon, his brother Gaenhyakdondye said, "We have indeed made an agreement, as you know, that we should forsake our families and our own lives in order to accomplish the purpose of this expedition. You know that each of us volunteered by 'notching the rod' to carry out that agreement. If we are to die here, we can do nothing to avoid such an end, but we must not break our resolution and compact to follow the path of the sun to the last. The only thing that is certain is that in the case of our death our careers would end here." His brother, Dehaenyowens, replied, "The situation is just as you have stated it; so then let us go forward to meet this people." At this they started toward the place where they saw the great crowd assembled. In a very short time the anxious travelers came to a standstill not far from the others. Looking around, they saw that the inhabitants of the settlement were preparing to witness a game of lacrosse, and that the players were already standing in their accustomed places.

In a short time the ball-game began and the vast multitude drew near as interested spectators. As soon as the lacrosse game was fairly underway there arose a great tumult; there was shouting and loud cries of excitement and approval inspired by the various skillful actions of favorite players. The great multitude rejoiced, and their new arrivals from the east were greatly delighted as well with what they saw.

During the game one of the players exhibited great rudeness in his manner of playing, striking right and left with his netted club without regard to other players who might be injured by his recklessness. Thereupon a person from the crowd, going up to him, said: "Stop acting so rudely; your style of play is too violent, because one who is rejoicing in the pleasure of the game does not perform this way. So do not do so again." Then the players at once resumed the game, playing as they never had played before. In a short time, however the player who had been cautioned to be more mild in his methods of play exhibited again his violence towards his opponents on the other team. At once, the man who had before reprimanded him went up to him again and said, "You must remember, I forbade your playing again so rudely as you were doing, yet you have disobeyed my request. As a result, now you shall rest for a time. You are simply too unkind and headstrong." Thereupon, seizing the ballplayer by the nape of the neck and by the legs and lifting him up bodily, he carried the offending player away. Not far distant stood a very large tree. In that direction the man carried the ballplayer, and having arrived near the tree he threw the youth against its trunk. Headforemost, his body penetrated the trunk, part of his head coming out on the opposite side, while his feet still protruded on the nearer side. Then the man quietly returned to the ball ground, and play was resumed. The game was continued until one side had scored the number of points required to win, and then the players again mingled with the crowd. Then the man who had imprisoned the rude player in the tree thereupon released him, with an admonition to be more mild in his style of play in the future. On his return to the multitude the man told them that it was time for them to return to their several homes, and they dispersed.

Source: *J. Curtin and J. N. P. Hewitt, "Seneca Fiction, Legends, and Myths," in the* Twenty-eighth Annual Report of the Bureau of American Ethnology *(Washington, DC: Government Printing Office, 1911), 611–13.*

As in many of the world's legends, a hero figure, or in this case a group of heroes, departs and journeys westward, if for no other reason than to satisfy their curiosity as to what happens to the sun each evening as it disappears. In this Seneca tale, their ancestral band find themselves, like Alice in Wonderland, in totally unfamiliar surroundings, where in comparison to what they had known, all things living—plants as well as animals—are larger, more beautiful, and, in the case of strawberries, more delicious—in short "a perfect world."

Of the several lacrosse practices touched on in this legend, one of the most important is the reference to the lacrosse stick as "the netted club." This places the action of the story unmistakably in the northeastern quadrant of North America, specifically the type of stick used traditionally by the Seneca. Only the Iroquoian variety could accurately be described as "netted," referring of course to the intricate rawhide webbing spanning the head of the stick. From Count Andreani's small illustration of an Oneida stick in his 1790 diary, we know that "netted" sticks have been used for at least 250 years (see figure 8). The Seneca identify with this stick so thoroughly, it was incorporated into their legends. The implication is that the stick goes back to mythi-cal times.

Other elements of the legend correspond exactly with the traditional Iro-quoian game, which the Seneca play: the use of some sort of village green (the "heath" mentioned in the tale) as a venue for sports events; the intermingling of players and spectators, possibly wagering on the game; the duration of the game to a prearranged number of goals needed to win; players taking up assigned positions on the field prior to the face-off. All these practices con-form to what we know of the traditional Indian game

Given the characteristic roughness of the sport, what sorts of rules, if any, governed the Indian game, and who enforced them? There is no documenta-tion supporting that a penalty box of some sort existed, as this story suggests, but in legendary time anything can happen. The removal of the offensive player by impaling him through a tree trunk is a clever supernatural means, however extreme.

Indian legends were told by elders to express social ideals, present heroic role models, and describe proper behavior. It seems that the removal of the player for slashing is meant to stress to the storyteller's audience that how-ever rough a game might be, one should be playing it for the sheer enjoyment of the sport, "rejoicing in the pleasure of the game." Rather than trying to inflict injury on one's opponents, there should be consequences for unneces-sary roughness.

VIOLENCE AND INDIAN LACROSSE

Before regulations were in place, wrote George Beers in 1869, "the best men were noted for maiming others and following the ball in raiding fashion, 'seeking whom they might devour.' That was in the days of no government [rules], when clubs were seriously considering . . . attaching surgeons and purchasing ambulances."* Beers was contrasting unruly Montrealers' playing style to that of the neighboring Mohawks.

An image persists of the Indian lacrosse game with scores of players doing battle and leaving a field full of dead and wounded players. Although there were occasional deaths connected with Indian lacrosse, almost all of them

---

*W. G. Beers, *Lacrosse: The National Game of Canada* (New York: W. A. Townsend & Adams, 1869; Montreal: Dawson Brothers, 1869), 44.

resulted from postgame fighting rather than violent behavior during play. This was particularly the case where large amounts of money had been wagered on the outcome, such as happened in 1845 when the Cherokee teams from Tallulah played Lufty before several hundred spectators. Thousands of dollars worth of goods and livestock were at stake, so tensions were high. They exploded when the Luftys ran two horses onto the field in an attempt to cut off a Tallulah player about to score the winning goal. The player, however, was able to run around the first horse and jumped onto the back of the second. In the fight that broke out, three players were killed and so many injured that some of them remained on the field for days. Another postgame free-for-all is recorded following a Creek-Choctaw game in 1790 to determine which tribe would have territorial rights to a large beaver pond. When the Creek were declared winners, Choctaw warriors attacked them; 500 were reported dead by the next day.

Occasionally when feelings were high, violence would erupt during a game. During an early-twentieth-century game between the Cherokee towns of Eufaula and Abilika, general fighting broke out at the very first face-off. It lasted three hours, when the county sheriff and his deputies were called in but were unable to break it up. Games of the Creek Indians were known to dissolve into melees. Played all day, the contests might last until nightfall, unless fighting broke them up. Basil Hall (a British Royal Navy captain visiting North America) in 1828 left a Creek game before it was finished when the Indian agent warned him that the players' level of excitement would still be so high, Hall could expect to see them start smashing heads with their sticks.

Once non-Indians took up lacrosse in the mid-nineteenth century, it seems that they played an even more violent game. Evidently the white man introduced into the game elements of violence unknown in the Iroquois style of play they had learned from the Mohawk. In authoring his "Rules of Lacrosse," Beers was attempting to "civilize" as much the excesses of whites as of Indians. He was intent on ridding lacrosse from injurious practices that had slipped into the middle-class white game of Victorian Montrealers. Among other things, he wished to curtail swiping and slashing with sticks and the wearing of spiked athletic shoes. A chief from the Caughnawaga Reserve complained to Beers about the injurious nature of white play—smashing heads, cutting hands—pointing out that the Indians could play all day without inflicting such injuries; the Mohawk concluded by saying they only did so when drunk. Mohawks not only considered slashing another player "a mark of bad play" but had developed specific rules against holding or tripping. Whenever such an infraction happened, the game would be stopped and resumed with a face-off held at the spot where the offense occurred.

Lacrosse infractions were recognized by many tribes, and they had rules and regulations and referees appointed to enforce them. In the mid-nineteenth century the Choctaw outlawed head-butting; violating the rule would draw a five-goal penalty. Cherokee team managers might withdraw a player whose playing was felt to be too aggressive. Game officials were usually drawn from village chiefs or other respected elders to settle disputes on the field. In Bossu's mid-eighteenth-century report on Choctaw performance, he insisted the players never became angry; furthermore, referees would remind them before the game they were playing for sport, not blood. Referees on the Cherokee fields carried long willow switches. If a pair of opponents decided "to go at it," the official would hold their sticks for the duration of their scuffle. If they seemed to prolong the wrestling overly long in his judgment, he would begin to whip them with his switch to get them back into the game.

INDIAN GAME COMPOSURE

John Pope, traveling through the South in the 1700s, was impressed by the stoicism of Creek players. "A dislocated Joint or Fractured Bone is not uncommon: Suffer what they may, you'll never see an angry look or hear a threatening word among them."* Indian lacrosse players by all reports were unusually restrained in their play. Iroquoian people use lacrosse as the ideal training grounds for their young boys, teaching them discipline and composure in the face of strife. In this way, the game provided socializing benefits. Some scholars have argued that this goes back to the days of warfare, where composure in battle was a means of demonstrating bravery, hence the concept of "braves." Cayuga boys in learning lacrosse discover how to channel aggression, allowing them to avoid becoming "burnt knives," or delinquents.

Deliberate game injuries were not unknown. When they did occur, they led sometimes to disastrous situations, such as an incident in the 1794 game between Seneca and Mohawk that nearly led to war. Some teams developed

---

*Cited in John R. Swanton, "Social Organizations and Social Usages of the Indians of the Creek Confederacy," *Bureau of American Ethnology Bulletin Number 103* (Washington, DC: Government Printing Office, 1928), 458–59.

reputations as "dirty" players, like the "mean" warrior clans playing men of the chief clan in Yuchi ceremonial games. Violence could of course surface when individuals had some particular grudge to settle. William Warren, an Ojibwe historian of his tribe, for example, describes how during a peace conference between the Red River Ojibwe and the Yankton Sioux, a Dakota player who had survived the battle of Long Prairie, Minnesota, slashed an Ojibwe opponent for some trivial reason. Open violence between the two teams (traditional enemies) was averted when the Sioux chief ran onto the field, separated the two players, and upbraided the Dakota player. George Beers made special note that injuries among the Mohawk were rare and that any rough manner of play had been learned from Canadians. Most Indian injuries, he writes, took place near the goals, due to the Indian habit of "bunching" their defenders whenever a goal was threatened.

General Indian composure in lacrosse can be contrasted with the violent behavior usually of nonnative Canadian fans. In British Columbia the Vancouver–New Westminster rivalry was intense. Vancouver fans once tossed New Westminster players over the park fence at one game, and a Vancouver coach being pelted with rotten eggs pulled out a pistol and began firing at the New Westminster crowd at another. When New Westminster played Nameimo, Peter Black recalled, "Many nights we walked out of the [Nameimo] Civic tightly bunched into a ball as one group, because the New Westminster fans would be waiting for us outside our dressing room . . . taunting us and throwing things . . . On some nights we had to walk out as a single group, clutching each other tight, all the way down to the ferry dock."*

*Cleve Dheensaw, *Lacrosse 100: One Hundred Years of Lacrosse in B.C.* (Victoria, BC: Orca Books, 1990), 45.

Conclusion

Despite the sporadic disappearance of Indian lacrosse in the past under pressure from missionaries and government authorities, the game continues to be vital in many American native communities. Regrettably, the Great Lakes game is extinct, although a handful of dedicated adults have made attempts to revive it at the youth level. The southeastern game flourishes among the descendants of Indian people who traditionally played in Oklahoma, Mississippi, and North Carolina; they perpetuate the two-stick version of ball play and follow the old "toss-up" practice for face-offs.

The northeastern, or Iroquoian, game has never lost its impetus and is very active in New York and southeastern Canadian leagues. Except for ritual games, Iroquoian teams play mostly the box version of the game invented in the 1930s by Montreal hockey entrepreneurs. Informal "pickup" games can be seen on any Iroquois reservation. A few stick makers in the Northeast bravely continue the tradition, but since the advent of the synthetic stick about 1970, their market has shrunk to almost nothing. Talented Iroquoian youth have been recruited by Division I and III teams, some of them developing into leading players in college ball. The best of them (Delby Powless, Marshall Abrams, Gewas Schindler) have gone on to play professionally in the National Lacrosse League, and that league's Buffalo Bandits are coached

FIGURE 14.

"He then took his ball-stick and commenced running up a big mountain, whooping as he went" (from the Ojibwe legend "Puck-wudj-Ininees, or the Vanishing Little Men"). Adam Songetay, a runner in the 1968 Healing Circle Run, sponsored by the Great Lakes Indian Fish and Wildlife Commission (GLFWC), carries a "walking stick"—a relay baton modeled after the traditional Ojibwe lacrosse stick.

Photo courtesy GLFWC

by Darris Kilgour, a Tuscarora. The creation of the Iroquois Nationals team and its acceptance in international competition has done much to remind fans of the game's native origins, over a century after Indians were excluded from playing on white teams by the 1869 regulations.

Even where the Indian game has died out, images from it are retained symbolically. The traditional Ojibwe stick makes its appearance as a cultural icon and expression of cultural pride in unusual off-the-field places—powwows, for instance. In these events, as part of their dance regalia "traditional" male dancers usually carry some item from the older culture—a war club, an eagle wing, a tomahawk, or an ornamental pipe; occasionally one will hold a lacrosse stick as his trophy. In the course of a song, when the singers perform their "honor beats" (four heavy drum strokes), the men raise these items heavenward to honor the spirits. The powwow's opening Grand Entry of dancers single-file is led off by war veterans carrying flags. In addition to Canadian and American flags is always the "Indian flag"—a long fur-wrapped crook, adorned with eagle feathers and dating back to warfare days. It was modeled after lances warriors took into battle and speared in the ground to indicate a position behind which they would not retreat. Recently, an addition to the Grand Entry parade of flags was someone carrying an enormous Ojibwe lacrosse stick painted red, the color of war. The Lake Superior Ojibwe have begun sponsoring spiritual "runs" meant for healing. At one of them a young St. Croix Ojibwe, Adam Songetay, carried a "walking stick" modeled after the Ojibwe lacrosse stick. The image he presented mirrored a character in the Ojibwe legend of the "Vanishing Little Men" who "took his ball-stick and commenced running up a big mountain, whooping as he went" (figure 14).

The colorful lacrosse legends of the first Americans remind today's players of the centrality of the sport to the people who invented it. This rich body of oral literature has been passed down through generations, just as Homer's *Odyssey* was transmitted over time by storytellers. The legends demonstrate native pride in tribal history. By honoring ancestors and culture heroes through different lacrosse traditions and tribal stories, Indian people speak to their game's ancient appeal The fact that more than one tribe takes credit for originating lacrosse reflects its nearly universal appeal among Indian people east of the Mississippi River. The Menominee tell how Manabus invented lacrosse to avenge the killing of his brother, Wolf, by evil underground spirits. In the legend, the Golden Eagle brings the ball to be used, then invites all the other thunder spirits to play. This legend promotes the image of good triumphing over evil.

Because lacrosse is still a relatively recent sport for nonnative players, it has not had the centuries of play within which Indian athletes developed their many lacrosse rituals. But whether consciously or not, some young white players have adopted certain practices from the Indian game and even created their own rituals. University of Arizona player Tom Christian decided to continue his black under-eye markings to enlarge them in his own design as face paint, until coaches of other teams complained; his roommate, Brian Moore, also a player, had a tattoo put on his left shoulder copied from a photograph of a nineteenth-century Cayuga stick. Prior to the first face-off in today's nonnative game, it is common to see players in a huddle conclude their "fired-up" talk by raising all the sticks and banging them together—exactly as George Catlin painted the Choctaw doing in 1834—possibly a form of Indian taunting in ball play (figure 16).

Where teams have developed their own rituals, the practices seem deigned to express solidarity as part of becoming "psyched up" for action. One Minneapolis high school club team invented its own brief ceremony: its players in a circular huddle with arms over each other's shoulders would rock from side to side, slowly at first, increasing their tempo gradually, as the coach walked around the circle, slapping each player on the back, while chanting his encouragement of the team in call-and-response manner. They concluded this ritual with the familiar raising and banging of sticks together. Evidently, this performance was effective in unnerving opponents, as they defeated other teams with better players and equipment (shorts that matched, for instance). The same club team followed its routines regularly. Like Cherokee players "going to water" directly from games, the players all arrived at a particular restaurant and sang the National Anthem, for which they were rewarded with free food—much like an Iroquois team in the nineteenth century would find itself entertaining European audiences by performing a "war dance" following their exhibition game.

The image of the "noble warrior" is held in high esteem today by most players in recognition of the game's origins. This is in keeping with the romanticized characterization of the American Indian going back to Jean-Jacques Rousseau in the French Enlightenment at the end of the eighteenth century. Often the warrior image is portrayed as the stereotypical dark-skinned head wearing the splayed eagle-feather warbonnet. Although often exploited for

FIGURE 15.
Some players today extend and enlarge their under-eye blacking to form designs, not unlike the face-paint of Indian players, including one of the all-time leading attackmen for Syracuse, Michael Powell, in 2001.

Photo courtesy Syracuse University Athletics

commercial purposes, the image has also been honored by the lacrosse community to celebrate noted players from history. It has inspired the life-sized bronze sculpture of two Iroquois players manned in breechclouts fighting over possession of the ball on the lawn of the Lacrosse Foundation in Baltimore; it served as well as Fred Kail's model for the figure of a Mohawk player mounted on the *tewaarathon* trophy awarded annually—the Heisman Trophy of lacrosse.

Indian players, however, are well aware that the image has not always been so positive a one. They scarcely need reminding that a century ago white Montrealers in creating what we know today as "field lacrosse" were blatantly racist in their attempts to "civilize" the game by purging it of its more "savage"

FIGURE 16.

The University of Arizona men's lacrosse team (shown in 2005) (*facing page, top*) and the Johns Hopkins women's team (before a game with Ohio University in 2006) (*above*) lift their sticks in unison. Besides team solidarity, this pregame ritual demonsrates each team member's mental and emotional preparation for a game. It replicates a lacrosse tradition that George Catlin captured in a drawing of Choctaw players at Fort Gibson, Indian Territory (later Oklahoma), in 1832 (*facing page, bottom*).

Drawing from James Mooney, "The Cherokee Play Ball," The American Anthropologist *3 (April 1890): 113. Photos courtesy of Timothy Galaz, Tuscon, Arizona, and Will Kirk, Homewood Photographic Services, Johns Hopkins University.*

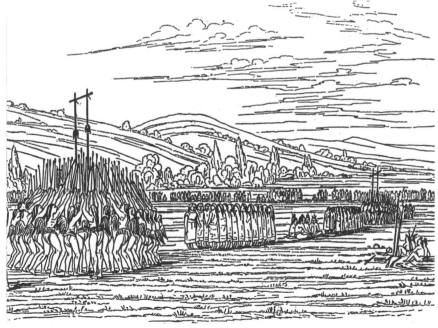

elements, as they described the style of Mohawk play. On occasion, native athletes today are capable of playfully "buying into" the earlier stereotype. Roy Simmons Jr., former Syracuse University lacrosse coach, relates an incident before a game on the road. One of his players in the 1967–69 seasons was a native, Freeman "Bossy" Bucktooth, an Onondaga whose sons later played for Syracuse (2004–05). At the time, the large, dark-skinned, muscular attackman had let his hair grow to unruly lengths and presented an ominous appearance. Simmons relates how this "scary-looking native with his 'steely look,'" implored the coach to let him be the first off the bus to jostle the nerves of their hosts, who would wonder how many more like Bossy were behind him waiting to emerge from the bus!

When the Mohawk Traveling College published its *tewaarathon* (the Mohawk word for lacrosse) in 1978 it was the first time that descendants of the game's originators had published their story. Prior to then, what was written about the game had been the work of newspaper columnists, academics, and anthropologists. Stressing the value of the oral transmission of their culture, the Mohawk researchers provided an illustration of an audience of children listening to a Mohawk elder telling traditional stories; presumably he is meant to be relating the story of the great game between the birds and quadrupeds, which the curators of *tewaarathon* included in their text. In recounting the legend, the researchers tell us, the elder is explaining the important role of community: "Our grandfathers told us that when lacrosse was a pure game and was played for the enjoyment of the Great Spirit, everyone was important, no matter how big or how small, or how strong or how weak."*

Just as Indian children could identify with culture heroes, following their adventures as related in these lacrosse legends, today's young players need role models. By identifying with such heroes as Red Horn as he defeats cannibal giants in a game of lacrosse, young Ho-Chunk Indians recognize the traditionally central role of lacrosse in their culture and come to appreciate how it is that the tribal athletic heroes of the past are remembered and celebrated. A dictionary of the language of the Kaskaskia Illinois Indians (circa 1720) has an entry reading, "they play lacrosse for the sake of the dead one."

---

*tewaarathon (Lacrosse): Akwesasne's Story of Our National Game (North American Indian Traveling College, 1978).

The Menominee hold memorial games to honor famous players. Mitchell Wakau sponsored one annually for his father, "Living in the Sky." Said to have been one of the fastest runners on the reservation, opponents used to assign four men to guard Wakau, "because, if he got the ball, it was considered to be already at the goal." Similarly, young Mohawk learn of legendary St. Regis player Angus Thomas, who has a street named after him and whose "heavy shot" once killed a man. Today's young nonnative players can look up to recent stars, like the Gait brothers of British Columbia, first at Syracuse, then in the professional leagues, or the three Powell brothers, also Syracuse and professional standouts.

Lacrosse is a great source of pride to young players today, despite the danger of its popularity being reduced to exclusivity, as an activity that is "cool." Oren Lyons, Faithkeeper at Onondaga and Hall of Fame inductee (see figure 12), emphasized the pride factor but stressed the importance of its communal nature: "There would be a winner and a loser, but that didn't seem to be important so much a point of the game as the celebration, the sense of community, the being together with pride."*

Fans and players alike have much to learn from the way Indian people have used the sport to channel aggression creatively. The legends make it evident how deeply spiritual was the Indian game of the past, how they credit the spirits with giving Indians the game and its equipment. The spiritual nature of lacrosse also helps to explain why Indians have over the centuries used it as a healing mechanism. Until recently, the Menominee played a ceremonial game to restore some ill person's health—a practice going back at least to the early seventeenth century, when the Huron ball play was likewise used to cure disease.

After the arrival of Europeans, smallpox wiped out large numbers of the Indian population. The devastation caused by smallpox had an equally undermining effect on the traditional role of the medicine man, whose powers and authority began to be questioned by his people. Still, they continued to use the game for its curative function: when the great Seneca prophet Handsome Lake was dying at Onondaga in 1815, they played a game for him, probably in an attempt to save his life. More recently, in 1990 in a Mohawk

*Cited in Robert Lipsyte, "Lacrosse: All-American Game," *New York Times Magazine,* June 15, 1986, 44.

community deeply divided over gambling issues, violence erupted leading to car burnings and shootings. Two years later their lacrosse players started a league to include both factions; eventually it was instrumental in restoring peace to the reservation.

As a group, these rich and colorful stories show the centrality of the game to native culture, and their plots tell us much about the environment surrounding the authors of the stories. Because the tales were used for their instructional value and moral lessons, they encode many traditional beliefs. For instance, "The Pale Moon" (chapter 3) tells that the moon is turned pale and its size diminished as a result of unfair play.

These 13 stories represent only a small portion of Native American lacrosse legends. Nor should it be assumed that they were isolated instances in the tribal oral repertoires. Not included here, for example, is another Ojibwe tale, replete with color and directional symbolism, which describes another "great game" (like the Eastern Cherokee, chapter 1), where the lacrosse teams are made up of all the birds—divided into those who fly south for the winter and those that remain. (The legend explains why.) Also, the plots of these stories—like all oral narratives—were subject to wide variation. For example, the "great game" between the birds and quadrupeds is cast in other versions as being between those creatures with feathers and those with teeth.

This volume of legends should help fill some of the gaps in our knowledge of the early history and composition of the game. In the details of their plots they inform us considerably about the environment and society of the storytellers and their audiences. In the details of the lacrosse actions we are given a glimpse of how Indians of the past played the game—even how they used their sticks. Although they don't give us as precise a description of playing skills as one might encounter in an issue of *Inside Lacrosse,* nevertheless we can readily envision the action in the Ho-Chunk game, where Turtle, having recovered the ball from the toss-up, is crowded by giants and, in a hurry to rid himself of the ball, passes downfield—only to have it intercepted by Martin.

Because these lacrosse legends wander freely into the world of fantasy, they entertain us as much today as Indian children of past centuries. Imagining ourselves back in the Wisconsin Woodlands a hundred years ago, we can laugh along with Ojibwe youngsters hearing about Wenaboozho sent sprawling and losing his carefully captured prey, or with Menominee children following the hapless Manabus as he races to escape the waves of Lake Michigan and the wrath of the gods he fired his arrows at, or with Ho-Chunk kids, as Red Horn's tiny human-head earrings rattle his redheaded giantess opponent when they wink their eyes and stick out their tongues.

Appendix

Mexican Kickapoo: Algonquian, *Northeast*
Miami: Algonquian, *Northeast*
Mohawk, *see* Iroquois
Ojibwe (Chippewa): Algonquian, *Northeast*
Oneida, *see* Iroquois
Onondaga, *see* Iroquois
Ottawa: Algonquian, *Northeast*
Passamaquoddy: Algonquian, *Northeast*
Potawatomi: Algonquian, *Northeast*
Saulteaux (Sault Ste. Marie Chippewa/Ojibwe): Algonquian, *Northeast*
Seneca, *see* Iroquois
Tuscarora: Iroquoian, *Northeast*
Yankton (Nakota): Siouan, *Plains*
Yuchi: Yuchi/language isolate, *Southeast*

Bibliographic Note

Despite its growing popularity today, when compared to games like baseball or football with widespread public appeal, lacrosse remains one of the least documented. This lack of historical attention has been addressed by Donald Fisher's *Lacrosse: A History of the Game* (Baltimore: Johns Hopkins University Press, 2002). As Fisher points out, many of the problems about our knowledge of the early history and development of lacrosse can be attributed to the fact that its American Indian creators, lacking written traditions, kept information in their memories and passed it to younger generations through oral tradition.

The main focus of Fisher's book is on the history of lacrosse since about the middle of the nineteenth century. At that time, upper-class Montreal amateurs adopted the game that was played by the Mohawk Indians on the nearby Caughnawauga and Oka Reserves. In the spirit of nationalism surrounding Canada's birth as a nation, they wished to make it the country's official sport by changing it into a "gentleman's game." In codifying their new "Laws of Lacrosse," they tried to sanitize the Indian game by ridding it of its "primitive" elements.

Most published work on lacrosse has been restricted to instructional manuals, handbooks with rules and regulations, newspaper accounts by sportswriters, and brief, often inaccurate, lacrosse histories included in larger works. With few exceptions, past scholars have been disinterested in the game, while lacrosse enthusiasts (primarily the socially elite) have preferred to chronicle the happenings of the sport (victories and losses) rather than to analyze it. Fisher's study corrects the lack of any serious analysis of lacrosse by addressing its history "within broad cultural and social contexts." His particularly insightful epilogue "Contested Ground" and his conclusion, "Ground Still Contested: North American Cultures and the Meaning of Lacrosse," should be required reading for all players.

Before Fisher's study, my own *American Indian Lacrosse: Little Brother of War* (Washington, DC: Smithsonian Institution Press, 1994) was limited to the history and composition of the Native American game as far as they could be reconstructed. As such, it is based on a wide range of anthropological publications, especially those of the Bureau of American Ethnology in its Bulletins and Annual Reports. Additionally, I consulted early writings of Europeans and Euro-Americans, beginning in the seventeenth century; these included reports from travelers, missionaries, artists, and the occasional member of European royalty wealthy enough to support a tour in the American wilderness and publish about it. My study is supplemented by field interviews with native players, stick makers, and coaches. Fisher's "Essay on Sources" and my own bibliography together represent the most complete listing of published and manuscript sources on the sport of lacrosse to date.

The first comprehensive treatment of lacrosse was in Stuart Collins, *Games of the North American Indians* (1890). Of the tribes playing the sport, the Eastern Cherokee have received the earliest and most attention, beginning with James Mooney. His article, "The Cherokee Ball Play" in the *American Anthropologist* of 1890, was followed by several volumes focusing on myths and sacred formulas. Lacrosse players owe a particular debt to Mooney as the first to photograph the game. Raymond D. Fogelson's critical analysis of lacrosse as a warfare surrogate in his doctoral dissertation, "The Cherokee Ball Game: A Study in Southeastern Ethnology" (University of Pennsylvania, 1962) is to date the most comprehensive treatment of any North American Indian sport. Another scholar focusing on the southeastern game is Kendall Blanchard in his publication, *The Mississippi Choctaw at Play: the Serious Side of Leisure* (Urbana: University of Illinois Press, 1981). A study of another Indian sport is Peter Nabokov's *Indian Running: Native American History and Tradition,* 2nd edition (Santa Fe: Ancient City Press, 1987).

The most up-to-date general reference work on Native Americans is the *Encyclopedia of North American Indians,* ed. Frederick E. Hoxie (Boston: Houghton Mifflin, 1996). Readers should also consult the two volumes of the Smithsonian Institution's authoritative *Handbook* series that cover roughly the eastern half of North America—the area where native lacrosse has been played: *Handbook of North American Indians,* vol. 15: *Northeast,* ed. Bruce G. Trigger (Washington, DC: Smithsonian Institution Press, 1978), and vol. 10: *Southeast,* ed. Raymond Fogelson (Washington, DC: Smithsonian Institution, 2004). Their bibliographies are both definitive and exhaustive.

A landmark publication, *tewaarathon (Lacrosse): Akwesasne's Story of Our National Game* (North American Indian Traveling College, 1978), is a long-overdue study by the descendants· of the inventors of lacrosse. It was researched and written in reaction to the fact that their game had far too long been controlled and regulated by the nonnative world; the work is, as Fisher aptly described it, "an attempt to reaffirm Indian cultural sovereignty over the sport." It is to be hoped that their publication will inspire other Native Americans to research and publish on the sport they created.

Oral narrative collections are plentiful, but Archie Green's *Calf's Head and Union Tales: Labor Yarns at Work and Play* (Urbana: University of Illinois Press, 1996) in its approach was particularly inspirational to the present volume. Three important nineteenth-century figures deserve our special attention. Crucial to an understanding of how today's field game came about, George Beers's *Lacrosse: The National Game of Canada* (Montreal: Dawson Brothers, 1869) is highly recommended. The product of this brilliant 20-year-old dentist is written in an engaging style, at times wonderfully whimsical. Although George Catlin's artwork should be approached with caution, he was a fascinating figure on the American frontier. For a good critical analysis, the insightful study by William Truettner, *The Natural Man Observed: A Study of Catlin's Indian Gallery* (Washington, DC: Smithsonian Institution Press, 1979), gives the approach of a cultural historian. Catlin's own two-volume *Letters and Notes on the Manners, Customs, and Condition of the North American Indians* (London: Tosswill and Myers, 1841; reprint, Minneapolis: Ross and Haines, 1965), which includes a number of his line drawings, is an enlightening account of the artist's journeys to a number of tribes in the West. Also to be recommended for its interpretation is Brian W. Dippie, *Catlin and His Contemporaries: The Politics of Patronage* (Lincoln: University of Nebraska Press, 1984). An equally intriguing individual was James

Mooney, who provided us our first lacrosse legend in print and whose 1888 photographs of the Eastern Cherokee game have proved essential to the present study. A fine, up-to-date biography of the anthropologist is L. G. Moses, *The Indian Man: A Biography of James Mooney* (Urbana: University of Illinois Press, 1984).

INDEX

Page numbers in *italics* refer to illustrations.